Season of Mercy

Lent and Easter

with

Catherine Doherty

Compiled and edited by

Marian Heiberger

D1595531

Madonna House Publications
2888 Dafoe Rd, RR 2
Combermere, Ontario
Canada K0J 1L0

www.madonnahouse.org

Compiled and Edited by Marian Heiberger

Cover painting by Heidi Hart

Design by Rob Huston

Layout by Rosalie Douthwright

New revised edition: March 25th, 2011

Library and Archives Canada Cataloguing in Publication

Doherty, Catherine de Hueck, 1896-1985

     Season of mercy : Lent and Easter / Catherine de Hueck Doherty; edited by Marian Heiberger. — New rev. ed.

ISBN 978-1-897145-12-8

     1. Lent—Meditations. 2. Easter—Meditations.

I. Heiberger, Marian II. Title.

BV55.D64 2011   242'.34   C2011-900824-6

This book is set in Bodoni, designed by Morris Fuller Benton in 1908–15, and based on typefaces designed by Giambattista Bodoni of Parma, Italy, at the end of the eighteenth century. Headings are set in Galahad, designed by Alan Blackman as a cross between Optima and the flat-pen writing of Friedrich Neugebauer, the distinguished Austrian calligrapher.

Contents

Book 3
The Easter Season

Book 4
Pentecost: The Holy Spirit

Book 5
Madonna House Customs and Traditions

Introduction

As foundress of the Madonna House Apostolate, Catherine Doherty gave daily talks to the community members, as well as guests who were living and working with them, at the community's Training Centre in Combermere, Ontario. This book is compiled mainly from transcripts of such talks; their context is the communal spiritual reading, which took place after lunch while the group was seated around the tables in the dining room.

Catherine usually began by reading aloud a passage from some author on a spiritual theme or an aspect of liturgy or Gospel life. She would then comment on the reading, her commentary comprising the major part of the "spiritual reading". Her talks were extemporaneous, and derived from her prayer and her own living of the Gospel. (Before Sundays and feast days, she read and commented on the Scripture readings for those celebrations.)

Catherine often began preparing the community for Lent immediately after the Christmas season. She understood well that we need to prepare to prepare—prepare for Lent, which is itself a preparation for Easter, which reminds us of our final passover at death. Her enthusiasm made other hearts catch fire; no one in the community wanted to miss Lent, let alone Easter!

For the community's Lenten spiritual reading from about 1970 until her final talks in 1982, Catherine read mostly from *Great Lent*, by Orthodox theologian Fr. Alexander Schmemann[1]. She felt very deeply that one aspect of her vocation (and that of her community) was

---

1   New York: St. Vladimir's Seminary Press, revised 1974.

to be a bridge between the Churches of the East and West, through love and knowledge of both traditions. The spirituality of Madonna House encompasses both.

Catherine understood the importance of celebrating our Christian feasts in ways that incarnate in daily life the mysteries we celebrate liturgically. The last section in this book describes some traditions she transplanted into Madonna House from the Russia of her childhood, as well as others the community has gathered from various sources. We hope that readers may find them useful in living more fully the new life that Easter brings.

These talks span a 25-year period from the late 1950s through the early 1980s and reflect changes occurring in the world, the Church, Madonna House, and in Catherine herself during those years.

The Editors

Preface

I am overjoyed and humbled at giving any commentary on the liturgy, but especially on this beautiful Paschal season, which repeatedly brings me to contemplate Christ's love. All Christians are called to contemplation, to a growing awareness that God is always with us, and that he loves us. This does not mean that we have to think about him all the time, but an open and loving heart can be aware of him without any effort, as time goes by. That is contemplation. And that is where the liturgy should lead us, with its psalms and the living words of Scripture. So I am glad to preface these reflections with words like contemplation, open heart, and an attitude of receptiveness.

My contact with theology is through prayer. By contemplating Jesus Christ, I come to know him, and I also come to know how to act. We acquire wisdom as we contemplate the Person who is himself wisdom, namely Jesus Christ. To me it is very simple. If I am in love with God then I can follow the teaching of one of the great Western Fathers, St. Augustine, who put it so simply: "Love God, and do what you will." That idea is like the Eastern idea, because if I love God, I will not do anything that he does not want me to do.

I am steeped in both West and East; I am perfectly at home in the Roman Catholic Church, but the other side of me well understands—not with my head, but with my heart—Eastern spirituality. We Easterners see theology in this way: my head goes into my heart. Western spirituality is more literal and defined. For those who are not familiar with the spirituality of the East, you need to understand that it has a twofold approach. We are exceedingly familiar and intimate with God, and at the same time we have a fantastic reverence for the transcendency of God. At the liturgy, for example, we feel this closeness to him and at the same time we feel that it is so fantastic, incredible, and awesome that he should come down from heaven for us.

We realize that each of us is a creature, one of the *anawim*, the poor ones of God, who depend on the Creator totally. Not as an abject servant, or in fear, but as one who rests his head on the shoulder of God and knows that of himself he is nothing. He does not have to hear Christ say, "Without me you can do nothing"; he already knows! This is very powerful in the Eastern spirituality.

I hope that you touch the spirituality of both East and West in this book.

From the writings of Catherine Doherty

Book 1

Reflections for Lent

God Loved Us First

Lent is a most important liturgical season, a time of preparation for the main event in the life of the Church and her members: the resurrection of Jesus Christ our Lord, the event on which rests our whole faith.

Throughout the year we realize what Christ has done for us, but in Lent we realize it more vividly. He has died on this terrible cross, and it is a death for love—He loved us so much that he died for us. Let us allow this reality to flourish in our heart. Let us concentrate on the fact that God loved us first; and when you really concentrate on it, it blows your mind that the Lord himself loved me. That is something so extraordinary that I cannot find words to express how he loved us. The greatest sacrifice a person can give is his life. Well, Christ did that, so in the very depth of your heart the reciprocal love that you have for God should blossom forth.

Lent vividly brings to us the love of God the Father, in that he sent us his Son. "Jesus held back nothing. He clung to nothing, and nothing served as a shield for him. Even his true origin did not shield him. 'He did not count equality with God as a thing to be grasped at, but emptied himself.' (Phil 2:6-7)"[1] Why did this man—who is also God—go forth preaching, when he knew that at the end of his preaching he was going to die a horrible death? Because he loved his Father, and for love of us, he obeyed his Father.

---

1 Johannes B. Metz, *Poverty of Spirit*, New York, NY: Newman Press, 1968

Begin with Desire

Lent is a spiritual journey. It has a particular spirit, quite different from any other time of the liturgical year, a spirit that tells you quietly and simply where you are going: to the Passover, the resurrection. You follow Christ across his whole life, you die with him, and you are buried in him, so to speak. This is the beginning of a new and everlasting life, and the "death of death". Because Christ died, he made us live. Lent is a time when we face these realities of our faith, and live them.

Preparation for Lent begins with desire. We exist to desire God. As St. Augustine says, "My heart is restless until it rests in Thee." In this is the preparation for Lent: touching a desire for God that is deep down in the heart. Desire is like a flame, it starts small and it grows. Lent should fan our desire for God into a bonfire.

The Incarnation has taken place. Christ was born in Bethlehem; he was a carpenter in Nazareth, where things were quiet before he began his public life. Then the mega-. phone of centuries brings to us his words. Some are powerful, at moments terrible: "Unless you leave father and mother..."; and at the next moment compassionate and gentle: "Has no one condemned you? Neither will I." Christ grows into his fullness in the three years of his preaching, right before our eyes.

In Lent we approach a threshold where this preaching will make way for pain and surrender. We approach a reality that he has enunciated to us and that we usually take lightly: "Greater love has no man than he lays down his life for his brother." We are going to enter the moment in which our brother Jesus Christ has laid down his life for you and me, and every human being who has ever lived in this world—for he is brother to everyone.

Each one of us can enter into his own heart and look for that desire for God. It might be a little flame barely visible, or it might already be a bonfire in us. Be that as it may, we are going to see how God loved us. This is what Lent is all about. Like Zaccheus (Luke 19: 1-10) we are going to climb a big tree of faith so as to watch that no word of those last weeks of Christ's life passes in one ear and out the other. His every act, his every word, must be enclosed in our desire, for if we are to fulfill our desire to see him when the door of death opens (and even before, for the Kingdom of God begins now) we have to imitate him whom we are going to look at.

This will require that we empty ourselves of many things, since the kind of fiery desire we must have takes a lot of space. It is not just a little kindling that we are going to ignite but huge dry wood. We must desire to empty every corner of ourselves of everything but this person called Jesus Christ, God and man, who died and resurrected so that we might see the face of his Father and meet the Triune God, the goal of all who have been born.

How does one get this great desire? The answer is always the same: prayer, fasting, and mortification. But prayer can be very simple: "God, I believe; help my unbelief." In that prayer God will send faith, and faith is the match that kindles desire.

"I am the way," says Christ. We must walk that way, believing and desiring him. Desire at one point becomes belief. Faith is reached by desire, and even in maturity, desire makes faith grow.

He who desires God already possesses him. The way to desire is to enter into Lent, to begin fasting not only from food, but from whatever leads us to run away from the new life God offers.

It is in his strength, and his strength alone, that we are going to make this forthcoming Lent a time of deep and thorough cleansing, a kenosis. It is in him and through him that we will put our house in order, so that we might go forth from it to put his order into the world. Above all, we must be open to the gifts of God, to the charity, the love with which the Father loves each of us— men, women, youth and children, old and young, every- one—this charity, this love that has been made manifest by Christ.

The Father desires, and so does the Son, that their love be expressed through the life of a Christian—a life of love, for charity alone can establish the kingdom of God. The whole of us, our body, our mind, soul, heart, emo- tions should be marshalled toward that goal. We have to prepare ourselves. Let Lent be a gathering of our ener- gies, a total engagement in a love that fully recognizes the love of the Father and the Son, and loves them back—and proves love daily and totally by loving our neighbor, right in our own house. If we want to love our neighbor, we help him to carry his cross. But we cannot do that until we are willing to carry our own.

The cry of our miseries, and of our dependence on God, blends with our confidence, love, and faith in him, for we know, we are sure that we will never be let down if we really trust in him. Christ says, "My grace is enough, my love is enough."

We may ask ourselves, how can I love and desire someone I do not know? How can I incarnate Christ's words, "Seek ye the kingdom of God and its righteousness" when I have no idea what the kingdom of God is? Or, if I have any idea, it is a very puny one.

The impact of his words, when we ponder them, is so strong for us that we block them. Now, why should I seek the kingdom of God first? Why shouldn't I seek self-fulfilment, money, comfort, security? We block his kingdom, we forget it and immerse ourselves in our busyness, our daily preoccupations. They are a kind of solace for us, as if by this busyness we would, in some sort of way, make it easier for ourselves to at least half-forget what Christ said. But this forgetfulness so often leads us into deeper failures, and even into sin; and lo and behold, our lives become "old" again instead of being renewed by Christ.

We can be just plain selfish, and if you are selfish, what happens? You concentrate on yourself, and life can become awfully dull. You might not know it, but you have spiritual arthritis before you have arthritis in your knees, instead of the newness of Christ and his victory over death, his victory of love over hate. We live as if Christ never came. We who know him, we live as if we did not; and to me that is the greatest sadness. I pray to God night and day, it is like a passion in me; all my desire is that people should know him, because once they know him, they will never let him go. And you find him in a very simple way.

You can find him in books; you can find him in all kinds of things. But the simplest way is this: stillness of body, stillness of heart, stillness of mind, and one thought: "Lord, come!" And you wait. The "wings" of your intellect are folded; your heart is wide open. You wait. And suddenly, when you least expect it, he is there! Now you have met, because he met you.

People talk about the pilgrimage to the Absolute. The strange thing about the Absolute is that he meets you halfway. But you have to have faith, the faith you acquired in baptism. Let us remember that Christ has come, Christ loves us, Christ has saved us.

Ash Wednesday

On Ash Wednesday we have ashes placed on our foreheads. What a curious Catholic custom. What does it mean, having ashes on your head? It means that you came from the earth and to the earth you will return. "Remember, man, that you are but dust."

Ah, but what dust! You are dust that is going to be one with God. Isn't that enough to make you dance, right in the middle of this ash business? We are not an ordinary dust—we are a dust that is going to be eternal, a dust that is going to be glorified, a dust that is going to be with God. So, let us prepare ourselves to receive that "dust" with joy—a joy based on discipline—and let us enter the corridor of Lent.

Lent is a time of going very deeply into ourselves, of really straightening the ways of the Lord. What is it that we have to tear out of our soul, by the roots? What is it that stands between us and God? Between us and our brothers and sisters? Between us and life, the life of the Spirit? Whatever it is, let us relentlessly tear it out, without a moment's hesitation. Let us be willing to surrender all that we have within ourselves.

Lent is a corridor that leads us to the face of the Father, the face of God. You cannot come heavily laden—you were born naked, and when you die you will come naked before God. His Son died naked. So, do not carry anything. You will take before God only that which you have given away. But you are not dead yet! So meanwhile, let things drop, really drop. Then you will enter Lent with a fantastic joy. For every time you drop anything pertaining to the wrong type of self-fulfillment, or to the adoration of yourself, or to all the things that clutter up your life, a sense of immense joy will come to you and through you.

Seven weeks are set aside every year for us to let go of the old and to enter into the new, because God is merciful. Now we can pass over from the old life that we led before Lent, into the new life after. This "passover" is a daily occurrence; it is not only during Lent. But Lent enhances it and makes you think. It concentrates you. It brings you into the heart of God. Lent is you and I, like St. John the well-beloved, putting our head on the bosom of Christ and hearing the heartbeats of God (John 13:21-25). When you hear the heartbeats of God, you change. We try to listen well to those heartbeats during Lent, so that we may not only repent and make our peace with God, but forgive all who have hurt us.

Let each one of us open his or her heart to God, and let him wash us clean, let him fill us with a hunger for him, and a thirst. Let him make us his own, so that when we come to Easter our joy will be beyond reckoning. All we have to do is pass from the old into the new. Leave behind the things that bind us away from God. Cut the cords with the scissors of love and go forth.

The Lenten Atmosphere

There is something very important that we can pray for, for each other. We cannot really get it by reading, but we can get it from our family or Christian community, through the Holy Spirit. It is a Lenten "atmosphere", which is created and into which we are immersed, as into the water in baptism. Faith comes by hearing, and the Holy Spirit must use somebody to speak. God has made us vehicles of the Holy Spirit for each other.

The Lenten climate that someone creates in a family deeply affects its members. This means that one has to be very alert and awake, because we are in a secular society. In Madonna House, which I consider a family, I have tried to create a Lenten atmosphere.

What does that mean, the Lenten "atmosphere"? For example, media today permeate our whole life. If it is not TV, it is the computer, or music—music as a kind of "background sound" instead of something we listen to. Fr. Alexander Schmemann says in his book, *Great Lent*,

> *[The] need for constant music reveals our incapacity to enjoy silence, to understand silence not as a mere*

absence of sound but as the condition for all real pres-
ence. If Christians of the past lived in great measure
in a silent world, giving them ample opportunity for
concentration, contemplation and the inner life,
Christians of today have to make a special effort to
recover this essential dimension of silence, which alone
can put them in contact with God. Thus, the problem of
radio and TV during Lent is not a marginal one, but
in many ways is a matter of spiritual life or death.

I suggest you drastically reduce your use of TV, radio, computers, and other media. What is involved here is the experience of Lent as a time for a silence created by absence of the world's noises to be filled with positive content. We need a break from the ceaseless hammering of the media. I suggest you feed your intellect by spiritual reading and feed your soul by prayer.

Let us examine our conscience further. We talk and talk, just to hear ourselves talk. We could use a little silence. Let us realize that the reality of Christ is not that we wear this or that garment, that we are this way or that way; but rather, "Do I love?" and "Do I show the face of Christ to the world?" The Holy Spirit is with us, but are we with the Holy Spirit? So, let us listen to what God has to say; he has said it to every generation.

When we are silent and recollected, we are mysteriously visited. That is the moment when Christ reveals himself to us. And then he tells us about himself, his Father, and the Holy Spirit. Then we receive our knowledge from God himself because we have broken our heart open, and we have interiorized ourselves. The Father, the Son, and the Holy Spirit have entered into us, and dwell there. And we have prostrated ourselves before the

Trinitarian God that dwells within us. In recollection, we listen, and God comes. And that is when we can begin to be a person of peace.

As Matthew 12:36-37 says, we shall be judged by our words. Lent is a time when we must think about what God's words in the Bible say. And out of this thinking, we must speak words of tenderness, love, pity, compassion, and gentleness, because we are men and women of faith; we are Christians.

Fr. Schmemann says further,

Lent is the time to control our speech. To control speech is to recover its sacredness, to understand that sometimes the words of an innocent "joke", spoken without thinking, can have disastrous results, can be the "last straw" that pushes a person into despair. But our words can also be a witness.

A casual conversation across the desk with a colleague can do more for communicating a vision of life, an attitude toward other people or toward work, than formal preaching. It can sow the seeds of a question, of the possibility of a different approach to life, the desire to know more. We have no idea how, in fact, we constantly influence one another by our speech, by the very "tonality" of our personality. And ultimately men and women are converted to God not because someone was able to give brilliant explanations, but because they saw in that person a light, joy, depth, seriousness, and love which alone reveal the presence and the power of God in the world.

Isn't it incredible, doesn't it amaze you, that we really can "make up what is wanting in the suffering of Christ"?

11

Christ appeals to us until death. He comes to you and me, and says, "Help me to bring people to my Father. Remember, I am the way. I died for you. Help me!"

So many of us are in need of alms from the other. Often there are people around us who are asking for alms, and we do not notice it. I think that part of our almsgiving this Lent should be directed to listening to one another; and to having a little bit of intuition about one another. And to allow the gifts of the Holy Spirit to penetrate in regard to one another.

Seek God's Will

God speaks to us through the Bible. If you are humble, simple, and direct, and love the Scriptures as something that really comes from the mind of God to bring you to his heart, then the Holy Spirit teaches you to read them. A whole new vista, a new dimension opens before you, and you enter into a world that heals you, cleanses you, washes you, makes you whole.

In repeating the Word of God and praying with it, even when it seems monotonous, there is tremendous light. We are always attracted to something that is exotic, interesting; we do not want to dwell on something that we may not understand, or which bores us. And so we pass by a whole dimension of our own life. We are willing to absorb the Scriptures if they are put before us in a pleasant way. If not, we sometimes go to sleep, don't we? But man's heart cannot live in a void. As you are faithful to what at first appears to be a monotony, the Holy Spirit comes and you are silently visited by the Trinity, and they become your teachers of theology—teachers about themselves, that is. For who knows more about himself than God does?

Just sit down some time and write what Christ asks you to do—and what you are doing. I do that periodically, and I am utterly surprised how completely I fail in what God wants me to do. And I am trying, I am honestly trying to live and do God's will. Yet always I have an excuse, always there is something where I say, "Oh well, God didn't mean that." God meant it, but we do not want to accept it.

Very few people really come to God and say, "Here I am, Lord. Do with me as you wish." It is hard to do that. But especially during Lent, you can change, make a new sheet and write on that new sheet: "Thy will be done", and do it. You know something? We well know what Jesus wants us to do.

It is very important to make "what God wants me to do" an exciting situation instead of being bored. Always bring God into it; and to bring God is the most exciting thing in the world. To make your life more with him is beyond any excitement. And Our Lady is a person to whom we can always go to for help. We should ask her, "Help me to be what God wants me to be. Help me."

In Lent, we make a journey with Christ in his public life and especially in his passion, which should break all the walls of resistance that we have. How can any walls remain standing within our souls when the voice of Christ, with tenderness and love, echoes in our ears through the Gospels? How can we remain indifferent and not break the walls of our selfishness, and passionately love God back, when our ears are "sealed" by the sound of a soldier's hand striking Jesus' face? When clearly we hear the whistle of the whips endured for love of us, as they pass through the air before they hit his already torn flesh? When we hear his slow steps walking that mile from Jerusalem to Golgotha, laden with a cross for our sins? And finally, when standing beneath that cross we see him, bleeding and torn, lifted up on it for our salvation, out of love for us, his final proof of it, and remain indifferent?

Every day of this holy season of Lent cries out God's love to us, and for us. Are we going to begin to cry out our love back to him? Or are we going to hem ourselves into a sort of deadly prison, by deadly words—deadly words so short and so tragic: "Yes, but; Yes, if; Yes, maybe; Not now, Lord, a little later." Is it possible that we can do that after we have travelled this holy journey, especially the last mile of his public life and his passion?

Let us begin Lent with a firm resolution to do just one thing: abolish the walls of our self-centeredness and self-ishness.

He resurrects—all this is leading to the resurrection—but do we resurrect? Christ says, "Do you love me?" and we do not answer directly, like St. Peter did: "Yes, I love you, Lord." We say, "Maybe; perhaps I will start loving you a little later." He asks us, "Are you going to follow me?" "Maybe, perhaps a little later."

This is the season when we hear the nails being put into his hands because he loved us. He did not say, "Maybe, perhaps." He just said, "I love you, and the proof is that I am dying for you." That is all.

And we look at him and say, "Well, thank you, Lord, that was nice of you, but don't ask me to do that, ok? I want something gentle. I want something according to my idea of how I should love you, not yours." If we had the guts to say, "Lord, your sayings are too hard and we will not walk with you any more," there would be no compromise. We cannot say, "Maybe." We can choose what to say: "We leave you" or, "We stay with you."

Learning to Love

The fall of Adam was a *felix culpa*, as the Latin used to say, a "happy fault", for it brought us Christ. Christ has come to take our sins away and reconcile us to his Father. We have a "door" and we have a "way", and if we pass through that door and we walk along that way, we shall see the Father. Christ is our brother; he is the brother of everybody, and so that makes us all brothers and sisters.

Jesus Christ made us brothers and sisters of one another and that is the tremendous essence of this thing called Christianity—we are followers of Christ, baptized into his death and resurrection. We preach the Gospel with our lives, or should, if we are Christian. (We can also preach it with our mouth, but the best way of preaching is with our lives.)

What is that Gospel? To love God with our whole mind, heart, soul, and strength; to love our neighbor as ourselves. Do not ever forget the "ourselves" business. You cannot love me unless you love yourself. If you despise yourself, if you do not care for yourself, you despise God's creature. You cannot love God either, if you do not love yourself. To put it another way, if you cannot love God and yourself, then how can you love me, your neighbor?

So please start loving yourself; and stop feeling guilty, miserable, and unloved, because there is not a human being who is not loved. God said, "If your father and mother desert you, I shall be father and mother to you." Let us face this fact, and do not let us feel that lonely. We are never alone. We are always in God. It is fantastically exciting to be in God, the Father, the Son, and the Holy Spirit. Christ our Brother, God our Father, and the Spirit moving us with his breath—all draw us like a leaf in the fall, up into the sky. Up into adventure. Up into loving one another. Guiding us with a golden thread of love. We can change the world.

He said, "By this you shall be known as my disciples, if you love one another as I love you." Get the picture: he wants us to love one another as he loves us, and he gave us an immense gift to do so, his grace. Why don't we start?

So we say that we should love one another. Well, that is fine and dandy. But how do you love one another? Unless you share of yourself, you are not loving anybody, least of all yourself. What I mean is this. I am kind to someone, and I say, "Oh, I just love you." But I never tell them what is in my heart. I never share with them who I am, or what I am. I do not allow them to come near me in a spiritual way. I am not talking about sharing my sins or emotional crabbiness, no. I am talking about that something that makes a person a friend.

We walk as if on eggs; we are always looking at the other person and saying, "What is he going to think of me if I tell him this and this?" Or, "If I tell them all that about me, well! I want the respect of my peers." When you do not share yourself, you also do not share God. To proclaim God and the Good News in a thousand ways, against ridicule by one's own group, is not easy. It is exceedingly difficult—it tears you apart, it leaves you mangled. But it has to be done.

If you allow sloth to come into you, you are not going to proclaim anything. Sloth is dissipation of our energy. It is also not being able to see the whole; it is the inability to have broad vision. How many people understand sloth in this way, have been given the real meaning? They think it is just laziness, whereas it is the negation of a whole vista of spiritual life into which we must enter. A vision of spiritual life is demanded; and we do not want this kind of vision that makes us change from the inside out. It is difficult and painful. It demands change; it demands letting go of security. And who wants to let go of security? We could really turn the world upside down, but we do not, because we are still being busy about ourselves.

Humility is a virtue that allows people to be open with one another, because the humble one has nothing to hide. So humility leads to openness. Let my life be known as it is, for whatever I have done or whatever I have been, I am a saved sinner. I have sinned many times, alas and alack, and I have this and that fault, but that is about the situation of everybody. So, why hide it? There is nothing to hide.

Humility is also a useful antidote for one's poor self-image. Humility takes off the masks we put on to hide ourselves. In humility, men and women can stand before each other, before everybody, as they are. You are not going to worry if people see you as you are. That is humility; and it goes into every corner of our lives. It is not one of the super-virtues like martyrdom that happen to one person in a thousand. It is a daily virtue, a very simple virtue. It walks along with us.

Only to the humble does God reveal himself in the Holy Spirit. If we do not humble ourselves, we shall not see God. Humility is the light in which we may behold the Light, which is God. As the psalmist says: "In your light, we shall see light."

Now let us get down to our everyday life. Humility is truth, and the truth recognizes itself very simply, if with great difficulty. There is no denying that to be humble is to almost tear oneself apart. It is, for instance, to accept true criticism of oneself with joy.

Pontius Pilate asked a lot of questions of Christ, and Christ did not answer. When Pilate said, "I have the power to crucify you and not to crucify you," Christ answered that he really did not. "You would have no power over me at all if it had not been given you from above." (John 19:10-11) Nevertheless, Christ accepted that he would be crucified.

How do we deal with being falsely accused? I can simply say that if the person really knew me, they would see true faults to accuse me of. There must be in our hearts a knowledge that accusations usually fall short of who we really are.

Why is it that humble people do not justify themselves? Because Christ did not justify himself. It is so very dark where Jesus sits. You stand at the edge of humility, you look down, and it is bleak and black and difficult to move into. There are no stairways, only a ladder into that virtue. But it is a strange virtue: as you go into it, it strips you down, and it washes you clean. When you emerge at some other side, you are another person. It is part of the repentance that we go through before God during Lent.

In Lent we should also ask God about the *humiliati*, as I call them. There are amongst us many persons who are lowly, and whom God seemingly has chosen to be over-looked, neglected, passed by. With a little nod of our head, we sometimes offer them a few alms of words when we are not too busy. But these people are our blessings when they pass through our lives.

We should seek out the shy ones, the ones that are frightened by life, the ones that have been beaten down by life.

For this is a true approach to Lent: not only to fast but to humble yourself, to know what humility is, to accept truth—which means to accept every "pain" that comes your way—and to forgive each nail of the hobnail boot that might crush you.

We need to drop all desire for others' approval, because the God we follow had no approval. There he is, cruci-fied—the consequence of the "disapproval" of man. That is what man did to his God. Are we going to repeat this crucifixion by our picayune little worries about being approved by somebody? Lent is a time to drop such things. Who wants to be approved? The ones who do not want to follow Christ. The ones who want the approval of people, people who are really unimportant.

Lent is the time of renewal and repentance, a time for change. Is it the time to have a wrong image of yourself?

You are the image of God and if you have a poor image of yourself, then you desecrate his image. That is not how one wants to walk through Lent.

What did Christ take away from us on the cross? Our shame. He has taken our sins away: mine, yours, and those of generations to come. By his crucifixion and resurrection, God has taken away everyone's sin.

Most of our sins, strange as this might seem, come from the fact that we do not love ourselves. We do not love ourselves when we do not realize that we are creatures of God who come from his hands. We do not enter into the orbit of God. A Christian puts his hand in Christ's hand, walks in step with him, and thus does the will of the Father.

When I do not love myself and therefore cannot love humanity my brother, I do the opposite of God's will. I do my will, and in doing my will make myself an idol before which I stand and worship. We have to begin seriously to think about truly loving ourselves. It is so intensely important. Love your neighbor as yourself. The shame of sin, which God took away from us, stems in many ways from the fact that we refuse to love ourselves. When you have accepted yourself you will be free, because when you accept yourself, you accept Jesus Christ. I think the greatest work that we have to do in this civilization is to accept ourselves as lovable.

I Give My Life

How much do I love? How often in my life does the pronoun "I" disappear, replaced by the words: they, we, he, or she? In this we have a very simple yardstick of love. Let us say a thought comes into your mind: "I want to do this." If it is something God would like you to do, go ahead and do it. But if not, erase it and keep on erasing it. The word "I" will disappear.

Let us think about forgiveness and about throwing ourselves on the mercy of God. In the Byzantine liturgy we often say, "Lord, have mercy!" One of the accents of the Eastern Church is an immovable faith in the mercy of God. We know he loves us, no matter what we do. We know that he loves us, not because we are good, but because he is good. Isn't that exciting?

You and I have heard the voice of Christ across the centuries saying, "Greater love has no man than that he lays down his life for his fellowmen." It is a joy to do that. Let us think to ourselves: I can give my blood for others and mix my blood with God's blood, in a sense. Because he gave his blood, his life, I can do it too, again and again.

Can you imagine how many today are following in the footsteps of Christ? There is a narrow road going upward to Christ. Some people walk it in a zigzag, going this way and that, and eventually coming back to the straight road.

Yet the Lord of History moves: God is present now; Christ is present now. He may come to one with this face and to another with that face, but with whatever face God comes, he beckons toward his real face. All these steps that people go through are ultimately leading to the one and only Lord and God who is the Triune God. It is beautiful to see people moving that way.

We Christians, of whatever denomination, must preach Christ. We must incarnate the Gospel, otherwise nobody is going to find the Triune God. God wants to work through us. We have to stop being hypocritical, compromising, and wandering away. Those of us who believe must now stand up and be counted, whether you are 60 or 16 or anything in between. I don't think God cares.

We are all apostles, those of us who are baptized in the death and life of Christ. We are people who are sent to testify to him by incarnating his Gospel of love. That is mingling our blood with his blood, and atoning for what we and others have not done.

Christ gave his life as a ransom for many. Are we ready to ransom the other, at the price not only of our death, but of our life? Sometimes it takes more courage to live than to die. To ransom Christ is to restore the dignity of men, to really see that every man has what he needs: food, clothing, shelter. To ransom Christ is to accept risks that amount to folly. They call it the folly of the cross but it is plain folly to most people. To ransom Christ is to open your heart to let everyone in. To ransom Christ is deep stuff: it is to change myself, so that I may truthfully say, "I live not; Christ lives in me."

Christ told the apostles of his pain and of some of his trials and tribulations to come. They did not take it in. It was a little beyond them, so one cannot accuse them of complete stupidity. They thought that they were going to sit at his right hand, and they said they were going to drink his cup. Yet when he was crucified, what did he see from the height of his cross? All those nice apostles running away; all he could see was the dust rising from their feet. Only one of them stayed there: John. The others did not drink his cup at that time.

That "cup" of suffering is offered to you and me. What are we going to do with it? There are ways of being crucified that do not involve rough wood or heavy nails, but a love beyond our capacity to love, which means a love that has been given to us by God, and for which we pray. Faith is the cradle of such love; it is the cradle of both hope and love.

If Christ's resurrection has no meaning for us, we may as well forget that we are Christians. His death on the cross did not make Christ anything—there were two others who died on the cross beside him. It is his resurrection that proves to us that he is God. Do you or do you not believe in the resurrection? Is it real, or is it fantasy?

When I believe in the resurrection I turn the other cheek, for I have to. If I do not turn that other cheek, I had better go deep into my heart and find out why. And maybe I will discover that I do not really believe in the resurrection. Because if I do believe, I will turn my other cheek.

Christ does not say to turn the other cheek as some kind of a symbol; he is uncompromising. He means, turn this human cheek; he means "accept". He means die for your neighbor. Our lives must "jive" with our beliefs.

Atonement

What is penance? Penance is an act of love. If there is no love, there is no need for penance. In fact, there could be no penance if there were no love.

Fasting and penance, which the Church calls mortification, have so much in common that it is difficult to separate one from the other. Fasting, in the natural order, helps to clarify the mind and soul. It gathers a person up and subjugates the appetites, of which sex is one, food another, sleep a third. There are many kinds of appetites, and one can fast from many things. There is also fasting from our own will, thus moving toward the ways that are Christ's, who through fasting and prayer led us to his Father.

It is one thing to control one's appetite; it is another to be exceedingly lavish in loving. For that is what penance is, in a sense. I see my brother in pain. I do everything to assuage that pain, like the Good Samaritan. I bring him into the inn of my heart, and do all the things that are needed to care for him. But after I have done that, I begin to think about the robbers who reduced that man to the state in which I had to help him, and into my heart comes a voice saying, "Love your enemies."

I say to myself, "I don't even know the names of those people. I don't know where they are from or where they are going. What can I do for them, or be for them?" In my heart, I hear the answer, "They have hurt this man." Now I can atone for them. I do not know their names, but I can atone.

When people in another part of the world are struck by disaster of one kind or another, you and I can send them money, and nations do too. But we who belong to Christ can also atone for them. Or perhaps I should say, with them. That is the next step of mortification and penance.

My brother is hungry. Shall I eat my fill? My brother is sleeping in the mire. Shall I sleep on a soft bed? My brother is in pain. Shall I refuse to bear that pain which comes to me daily through the difficulties of just being alive and living in any kind of community: marriage and family, village, or nation?

We are hair shirts to one another. I can be angry and hostile toward that one who is my hair shirt, and suddenly remember a woman giving birth in the dirt of slums. Then I can bear with love that which comes to me. Because there is something mysterious in this world that we cannot fathom. When I love enough to offer my body for another in a small way—perhaps by sleeping on the floor, eating just a little bit for awhile, and accepting such mortification and penances as come to each of us from each of us—something happens.

One of the most mysterious things that the Lord Christ left to us were these words of his: "Greater miracles than I, you will perform." This is one of the great miracles: that utterly unknown to anyone in a slum or hidden in a corner in Canada, I, by accepting such mortification and penances, help those people. How I have helped, in what way, I do not know. Only love knows, and love is God.

Love communicates itself to us. Faith is ready to walk in total darkness, dumb, blind, without hearing, for that is what faith is. If I am willing to move into the realm of faith because I love him who has given me faith, then in that fantastic warm darkness of faith I help the person in the slum, the one victimized by disaster. I may not know it. But this is the strange power of penance and mortification, this taking up of the physical burdens of others.

But there is another side. If I can atone for the ones who have sent the wounded man into that place where the Good Samaritan found him, if I can atone for the sins of others, I can also atone for my sins.

God is all-merciful. He does not ask me to atone because of fear. No. He asks me to atone because of love. He atoned for you and me on the cross. As St. Paul says, "You can make up what is wanting in the sufferings of Christ." Nothing is wanting in the sufferings of Christ, but because I am in love with God, I can pick up others' sufferings and carry them.

Christ has left to me the restoration of the world by his commandment of love—the restoration of the world politically and economically, and also spiritually. By entering into that task of restoration, I pick up his burden, which is the cross. Carrying the cross, invisible as it may be, is mortification, a heavy thing. It is penance.

So penance is for loving. Penance is for atoning. Penance is for identification. The only reason I can engage in penance, or desire to, is because I love. No other reason should ever be in my mind. I am not doing penance and mortification because I want to earn God's love or to deflate the wrath of God. There is no wrath; God is merciful. Nor do I have to do penances in order to appear a little holier than the other person. That would destroy me totally.

But faith is the cradle of love and the cradle of hope. Have you ever seen a man or woman whose eyes have lost, or almost lost, hope? Do you realize what you have to do when you meet those people? You have to render "first aid".

When we see hopelessness, we must give love. And love, like a fire, will bring forth hope. For we too can resuscitate others; even as Christ brought forth Lazarus from the tomb, so can you and I. Christ has given us this power. It is not my power, nor yours. It is Christ's power: "Men shall know that you are my disciples if you love one another, as I have loved you." I cannot love like God; neither can you. But I can cleanse myself. I can dispossess myself of myself, so that God can walk through me towards you.

God so loved the world that he sent his Son to atone for it. To atone is to put yourself in the place of another. In a Nazi concentration camp, Father Maximilian Kolbe offered himself to be executed by starvation in place of a Polish man who had a family. In doing so, he atoned for the sins of the Nazis. He substituted himself for another who was condemned to death, and in so doing he atoned for his murderers. Before God this stood as an act of sacrifice and atonement.

Atonement means reparation for a wrong or an injury. It means reconciliation of God to man. It is sewing up the torn cloak of Jesus Christ. Those who sin tear it, and those who atone, repair it. We all tear the seamless garment of Jesus Christ, but some of us are wonderful mend-ers. We can mend it. The greatest atonement is the cleans-ing of our heart.

There are people who love God exceedingly much, who enter into his passion very deeply, and who want to join themselves to that strange gift of atoning that God has given us. They have a deep resonance with what St. Paul says, that we "can make up what is wanting in the suffer-ings of Christ." This is a pure gift that God gives; Christ in his goodness allows us to make reparation. Lent is the time of turning the other cheek, the time of the infinite gentleness that Christ exhibited through his passion.

Mortification and penance are acts of love, passionate love in response to a Passionate Lover, that is all. So what we call mortification and penance are not really that. It is no use talking about penance and mortification other than as our passionate response to our Passionate Lover— God. It is the only thing that makes sense. Can your heart feel it? Mortification and penance are a passionate response of man to a Passionate Lover who is God.

The Sea of God's Mercy

It came to me that Lent is a sort of sea of God's mercy. In my imagination, it was warm and quiet, and inviting for us to swim in. If we did, we would be not only refreshed but cleansed, for God's mercy cleanses as nothing else does.

Then I thought of our reticence. I do not know if it is reticence, or fear to really plunge into God's mercy. We really want to be washed clean; we want to be forgiven. But these desires meet with something else inside. I say to myself that if I enter into that sea of mercy I will be healed, and then I will be bound to practice what Christ preaches, practice his law of love. And that law of love is painful, so terribly painful. There by that sea I stand and think. If I seek mercy, I have to dish out mercy, I have to be merciful to others. What does it mean to be merciful to others? It means to open my own heart, like a little sea, for people to swim in.

If we stand before God's mercy and drink of it, that means the *Our Father* is a reality and not just a prayer that I say.

"Our Father who art in heaven, hallowed be thy name. Thy kingdom come..." We like that part and have no problem saying it. But then we come to, "Thy will be done on earth as it is in heaven." And, "Forgive us our trespasses as we forgive those who trespass against us." We shake our heads and say, "Yes, it is Lent; it is true we should be forgiving everybody." But we do not like trespassers. If strangers come to use our beaches, we will say to ourselves, "What are they doing here? Why do they come to our beach?" It is not easy to make of one's heart a little sea of mercy for the other.

We need also to be listening to God's will. But we think, "Wait a second. *Thy will*—what does that mean?" As we look at the will of God, sometimes our hackles rise up, just to think of submitting to somebody else. But to submit to the will of God would be to put our toe into the sea of God's mercy!

Lent relentlessly shows us who we are, our true identity as Christians, what it means to be a Christian. "Blessed are the poor; blessed are the merciful; blessed are those who hunger for justice..." We recite the Beatitudes and each of them can make us move a little further away from the sea of God's mercy, because each demands so much of us, all of us.

Do we want to go into that sea of God's mercy, to be washed clean so that we begin to do the things of Christ? What is Lent all about? It is to go into some strange and incredible depths of our self, and there to meet the sea of God's mercy and, having shed all garments of selfishness and fear, to swim in it.

Take for instance the fear of ridicule. Did you ever stop to think what an absolute foolishness Christ is? It borders on—not mental idiocy, but a sort of passionate foolishness. Just think of a human being letting himself be crucified for someone else—in this case for the world. How high can the foolishness of love go? How deep, how wide? That is the foolishness he wants us to assume.

Lots of saints went about being ridiculed. Christ said to St. Francis, "I want you to be the greatest fool that anyone ever saw." And there was a little Franciscan brother, Juniper, who used to play seesaw with children; and people thought it funny for a man to do that. He did it specifically so that people would ridicule him. The Russian *urodivoi*—fools for Christ—loved to open themselves to ridicule. They wanted to play the fool to atone for those who call Christ a fool.

These are extremes of people falling in love with God so totally that they desire ridicule. But what about us?

Are we going to allow Lent to give us the immense gift of the Holy Spirit called fortitude? It is a gift that is little spoken of, and is neglected. Fortitude is courage, the courage of our convictions; the convictions that may invite the ridicule of others. But Christ said, "Who is not with me is against me."

Lent is here to remind us that the mercy of God is ours, provided we embrace his law of love. Provided we realize that it is going to hurt, and hurt plenty, but that the very hurting will be a healing. That is the paradox of God—that while you hurt, you also heal. And that is true healing.

The sea of his mercy is open before us. Lent definitely and inexorably leads us to it, and makes us think about what it takes to swim in it. This is a very great shortcut to God's heart.

Lent also reminds us that each of our hearts can be a sea of mercy and forgiveness to others.

Lent invites us to make a profound examination of conscience, to face our human condition as sinners so that we might, with our unseen and seen tears of repentance, wash off the stain of those sins that our weak nature constantly is prone to.

A cutting or an irritable word suppressed is a way to do penance fruitfully. The way we walk, sit, and talk, the expression on our faces, all these can be controlled; that is penance that is fruitful and pleasing to God. Such inward penances center upon *caritas*, love. To be concerned with others and forgetful of oneself is not easy, and is a fruitful penance that will bring so much charity and peace.

Deep down in the soul, in my soul and in your soul, in that center of what is a person, lies the essence of temptation. We think about temptation as something on the surface. Sex and all kinds of outward temptations come to our mind. They are important enough, but the real battle is inside, deep inside: to be alienated from God, or to be with God. Which is it?

Today, man puffs himself up. He gets bigger, wider, broader; he looks at God and says, "I went to the moon, you know. I don't need you. I can do all things by myself. I have knowledge equal to yours." This is a temptation to power.

The fight between the devil and me—the fight between the devil and God, in a manner of speaking—is within me, deep down below the surface. There is an awful lot that we do not even want to look at. We do not want to face pain, and so the last thing we look at is ourselves. But who eternally leads man away from his inner and true self into darkness, confusion, "un-reason"? He who was once light and is now himself darkness.

If I am self-centered, if I do not care about anyone else, and I want to put pornography on the screen, for example, I am making human beings subject to my desire. People who do that kind of thing desire money, and all the things that money gives, and they will exploit man in any way imaginable and possible.

If my life is not oriented toward God, nor aimed at eternal values, it will inevitably become selfish and self-centered. This means that all other beings will become a means of my own self-satisfaction. If God is not the Lord and Master of my life, then I become my own lord and master. I become the absolute center of my own world, and begin to evaluate everything in terms of my needs, my ideas, my desires, my judgments.

But if you have a respect for other people, if you have charity, which is the opposite of selfishness, you will not go that way. It is sometimes difficult to have reverence for the other, but it is absolutely necessary.

We have to enter deeply into the caverns, into the abysses of our soul, and take out from there all those little "packages" that are filled with our selfishness. Lent is the time of repentance; the time to take a broom and clean all that out. Repentance is the realization that I alienated myself from God and now I am running back to him, like the prodigal to the Father, knowing that he will receive me at all times, for his mercy is infinite.

Repentance and Forgiveness

Repentance is a powerful word. We should use it not only in Lent but constantly, because daily we commit acts, say words, have inward movements, that we are sorry for, wish we had not said or done, and in some way wish to atone for.

That is good. It is also good to know that sin is not the immediate cause of this or that calamity. Sometimes God sends us sorrow, trials, sadness so that we repent, do penance, and turn our face to him. At times it is very hard to understand that those calamities and tragedies can make us understand the love of God, and his tenderness and mercy shine with a new shine, better than ever. Let us be reassured and let us open ourselves to whatever God sends us. A supposed calamity changes into a benediction, into something we could offer to God. Let us look at things that way; it takes faith, but you pray for faith.

Let us be listeners of Christ's voice, and realize that what seems to us a tragedy is but a message, full and pressed down, of his love. Pain and suffering can lead to repentance and unite us again with Christ, especially if we have lost him temporarily.

Sin is turning my back on God. I walk away from God, into a deadly place, a Godless place, in which I look at mirrors, and in every mirror I see myself. Sin is the adoration of self, in a manner of speaking, instead of God. The Eastern Churches pray: "Turn not away thy face from thy servant, for I am afflicted! Hear me speedily, attend to my soul and deliver me!"

Listen and you will understand the starting point of Lent, the mysterious mixture of despair and hope, of darkness and light. I stand before God, before the glory and the beauty of his Kingdom. I realize that I belong to it, that I have no other home, no other joy, no other goal. I also realize that I am exiled from it in the darkness and sadness of sin: "for I am afflicted, Lord". Only God can help in that affliction, only he can attend to my soul. Repentance is, above everything else, a desperate call for that divine help.

Many are seeking, but what are they seeking? When somebody asked Christ, "Where do you live?" he answered, "Come and see." But we are all frightened when we get to know a little bit about Christ, because we realize that following him leads to crucifixion. Yet no one has understood that the moment you agree to be crucified on the other side of his cross, you do not feel any pain, and you are filled with joy.

We must face one thing: we cannot learn about God without immediately integrating what we learn into our life. It is not enough that we say, "I am going to change." No, it must be now, this very minute. What we learn about God has to be integrated into our life now, and thoroughly.

God is a very strange God. He calls you, "Come higher, friend," and between where you are and where he is at that moment there are, let us say, a thousand miles. Yet he says, "Come!" and then he vanishes. You wail, "I don't know if I am on the right road. I don't know if I should turn right or left." God says, "If you moved in security you would not believe in me, because it would be your security, not mine."

What is the security of this Man? Three nails. That is all. Would you like to accept those nails? We do not want to accept those nails, it is as simple as that. Yet we resist, and argue, in order to escape. The more I argue, the less I have to face. But the more silent I am in my heart, the more I accept. We read beautiful things, but unless we integrate them into our lives, we do not change.

We consider Lent a journey, a pilgrimage, to something very stupendous. Lent comes to us, not only as a season of penance, but as a season of repentance. And repentance is forgiveness also, because usually sins are interpersonal in the community of Christians—I realize that I have offended my brother and I am repenting of this.

Examining myself about the evil that other people have done to me, I turn my face to God, and I see how he forgives me every minute of the day. Through this journey, this pilgrimage, toward the light of Easter that renews us, I suddenly realize that because I have been given forgiveness, have tasted forgiveness, have bathed in forgiveness, experienced its warmth and its gentleness and its love so often, there is no problem for me to forgive the other.

That, to my mind, is repentance: I sorrow that I have not looked enough at Christ's forgiveness and love, so as to ask forgiveness of my brethren, and to forgive all of them.

The greatest penance that one can do is to really allow oneself to be cleared of hatred, and enter into the land of forgiveness. To forgive is literally to annihilate oneself. When I offer my forgiveness to another, nothing must remain in my heart. Not a shadow, not a speck of sand that remains inimical to the one I forgive. It is a totality of forgiveness or none at all.

To make a totality of forgiveness I surely must prepare myself by fasting, prayer, and penance. I am a sinner who has been saved, but the sin is with me; the shadows of sin are all over me and I must exorcise them. And the greatest tools of exorcism are fasting, penance and prayer. God has given us these three tools so that we might make ourselves clean inwardly.

Forgiveness must come from the very "belly button" of your soul. It cannot be superficial. It cannot be just emotional. It means to forgive in such a totality that, in a sense, whatever has been done to you does not exist, even in your mind.

Somewhere in our hearts there are always dead ends of human relations: something forgotten, something we have put away on the shelf or in the cavern of our soul. It may not show all the time, but it does come forth. All those dead ends have to be swept away into the lap of the Lord, or at his feet. We cannot enter radiantly into Lent unless we have forgiven.

Christ expects of us a peaceful approach to the other, no matter how hurtful that other has been, an approach like his own: "Father, forgive them, for they do not know what they do." I remember when the Communists shot a priest in Russia, an old man with a thin, reedy voice said, "Father, forgive them, even if they do know what they do." I understood then what total forgiveness could be. We can only understand forgiveness through Christ forgiving us. Christ who forgave his enemies while he lived, and telling us to forgive "seventy times seven".

The greatest thing I can do for anybody is to pray for them and really mean it. If I just say, "Lord, I have forgiven her; please look after her", that is not enough. The person has to be in my heart, in my mind, for a little while. Then I hand him or her over to God, clad in the white garment of my forgiveness. I forget them in the sense that I have forgiven them, but I remember them in the uniqueness of their person. Now they are just as they were before. It can be done. I think such love can do what is almost impossible.

✛   ✛   ✛

Easter, the Passover, [leads to] the end of all that is old, and the beginning of the new life, a constant passage from this world into the kingdom already revealed

by Christ. And yet the old life, that of sin and pettiness,
is not easily overcome or changed. (Great Lent)

A very good word, pettiness, meaning small things.
We say a person is petty when she or he makes a big fuss
over things that need not be fussed over, simple little
things. "Why didn't you put the salt where it should be?"
"The salt should be in the middle, don't you know that?"
"Well, for Pete's sake, you have it all around the place!"
And an hour later the two are at each other hammer and
tong, have forgotten about the salt, and are bringing out
a lot of other pettiness that is in their minds. In that way
we deeply offend each other.

God gives us a new life, and the liturgy helps us to
know it. Here is this beautiful, wondrous and tragic beauty; here is God dying on the cross. How does it feel to be
nailed to a cross with your hands and feet? How does it
feel? Think about it. Three hours he was on that cross
before he died. All this to give us a new life and make us
realize what that new life is all about. But we go around
looking for all kinds of gimmicks and we do not remember
why he died. We do not practice the new life. We do not
give it to others, which we are supposed to do, for each one
of us is an apostle, or should be.

You know, in the evening when everything is quiet and
peaceful, it is so hard to think of God crucified for nothing. You say to yourself, what can I do to make up for
everybody? And you find you cannot do very much.
People have to do things for themselves. It hurts. If you
love God it hurts. Yes, it hurts deeply to think that for
three hours he endured tremendous pain, which is for you
and me. All his life, his very incarnation—the fact that he
became man—all this is for you and me. And what have

we done with it? If you and I lived the Gospel totally and completely, what a different life it would be. How kind we would be to each other, how simple, how direct to everyone.

The kind of life we lead, you and I, is petty. It is not easily overcome and changed. Who wants to change this petty life for perfection? Perfection in itself is a discipline. Perfection in itself makes you listen. When you begin to know a little more about his Kingdom, you realize God speaks to you. All of us have heard his voice.

So many times I remind our staff: "The duty of the moment is the duty of God." In any life, it can be very hard to do the duty of the moment, because you are so attached to whatever else you are doing, in office or kitchen or wherever, and you do not want to change instantaneously. For example, to greet someone and get them coffee or tea and talk with them. You think, "Oh God, why should they come here and bother me?" It is simply because they have come, and you have to change.

Our inclination is to follow the pleasure path, the easy path. And then comes this Man and he says, "No, that is not where happiness lies. Happiness lies here, on this very narrow road. Climb." It seems absolutely idiotic, but it is not. You follow that road and you find freedom and peace. What a juxtaposition.

Lent is always associated in our minds with penance and mortification, usually with food and lack of it. But that is only a small part of it. Lent should make us face the issue: Do I want to live a life that, at the end will leave nothing to say, because I spent it doing what I wanted to do, as I wanted to do it, when I wanted to do it? I spent it in the service of myself, catering to myself?

We have to face ourselves and face God, and enter the school of repentance, which alone makes it possible to receive Easter as the end of the old and the entrance into the new.

✠   ✠   ✠

What does it mean to confess our sins? We speak of morals and ethics—a Christian does not do this, a Christian does not do that. But that is not all of Christianity; that is just a juridical approach to love. If you want to kill love, approach it juridically. It is relatively easy to say, "I have been angry", "I didn't say my prayers", "I committed adultery or fornication", and so on. Then I receive absolution and feel as clean as if I took a sauna bath, instead of a cold water bath without soap. That is what it amounts to.

Our confessions can be superficial and not go deep enough. If they are superficial, we have not really gone into the caverns and caves of our souls. We have wrapped up a lot of things, and stuck them on the shelves of the caverns, when they should have been brought forth. But we let them be, and like splinters they fester in our souls because we are not in truth and we have left integrity behind somewhere.

We are pilgrims of the Absolute, whether we realize it or not. When you begin to be a pilgrim of the Absolute, you want to change everything round about you. It takes long pilgrimages and much pain to find out that the first thing you have to change is yourself. Lots of people never get started, because they do not even realize that they are in an alien country, not in their eternal home. Many find it out very late, although of course, with God, it is never too late. For as long as we are alive, we can say, "Lord, have mercy on me," and he will save us; the Lord is compassionate and merciful to sinners. After we are sorry for a sin and turn to God, it becomes a glorious fault.

The East weeps over its sins because they are an offense against God who is love, against charity, and against one's fellowmen. For when I commit a sin, be it hidden in the dark recesses of my life or wherever, I sin against the whole Body of Christ, against all the people of God. No matter how hidden my sin, it reverberates across the rest of the world. For I am so deeply united with all of mankind, that what I do affects the whole world, and what I do not do also affects the whole world.

Let us stop for a moment and think what has been given to us by the incarnation, death, and resurrection of Our Lord: a new life! It is so fantastic; with God, every moment is the moment of beginning again. At any given moment your life is renewed. The light of repentance, the "Lenten Spring", has come. For this we pray. The moment we accept this repentance, the new life is in us. We are so lucky.

Our sins that are past, why even remember them? God has forgotten them. Why is it that we want to remember them? A forgiven sin does not exist in the mind of God. God is not a stingy forgiver who remembers our sins for the rest of our life. The mercy and forgiveness of God are infinite.

To Fast

Often during Lent, my mind turns to the reading from the prophet Isaiah that ends with the simple question: "Is this not the sort of fast that pleases me?" (Isaiah, ch 58) God evidently wants a broken, humble heart, because he says, "Rend your hearts and not your garments." God wants not so much a giving up as a simple giving. In order to really have an open and humble heart, to give lavishly of food, love, shelter, tenderness and compassion because of this humble heart, one must give up oneself. To fast the way the Lord wants means a total surrender of self to the other and for the other.

The Lenten season is a good time to examine ourselves. Perhaps food is not our god, yet we can worship our will, which feeds our ego out of all proportion. Perhaps in the depths of our souls we might be unforgiving, hostile, angry. These are shameful things, if directed toward our neighbor. Maybe I am not too concerned with things of the world, but very much with "my thing", my desires, and very little concerned with other people's needs. Lent is the time to find out, because when we have broken and opened our hearts, God comes.

What is a broken, humble heart? There is a story in the Old Testament (1 Kings 17:7-16) where a prophet went to a widow who had only a little oil and a little flour. He told her to make him a cake from it. She gave it all to him and as a result her oil lasted her a lifetime.

Have we got a heart of stone? Do we need a mallet to break it? If we do not have an open heart, we must break it open with some tool or instrument. Then the oil of love, tenderness, compassion, acceptance of the other as he is, watchfulness and alertness for the other, will pour out of us, like oil from the pitcher of that widow of Zarephtha. The oil will never run dry, and the size of a family will not be a concern, because there will be enough love, tenderness, and compassion for everyone who comes.

Such are the fastings that God wants. I give up myself without ever forgetting that I must love myself. And I love myself by giving of myself. "Greater love has no man than he lay down his life for his brethren." So if I lay down my life for my brethren, I fulfill the second great commandment: "Love your neighbor as yourself." I am loving myself rightly when I am laying down my life for the other.

It is such a gentle thing, that giving up—adjusting to what the other wants, not what I want or am interested in. In giving gladly to others, a ripple like sunshine or moonlight on water passes through your life, like a golden or silver thread. And you are not worried about anything. Who is ever worried when they are in love? Rather simple, this "fasting" for the Lord. Simple, but, like all things of God, immense. That is the paradox of the Lord.

Of course, in trying to have a broken heart, it does not do any harm to abstain a little from food and a little from drink—to do a few penances and an awful lot of praying. It helps!

It is so important, so vastly and compellingly important that we return to fasting. Fasting has a power; Gandhi's fast changed the face of India. We might change the picture of the world if we "indulged" in fasting, and prayer. These would also reveal to us the will of the Father.

It is a strange thing that when you enter into the world of fasting, a great peace comes upon you and at the same time, a great restlessness. It is one of the moments in which God and Satan fight within your soul. At the end of a day when you have had only bread and water, coffee, or tea, all kinds of thoughts about food come to mind. The first temptation comes from Satan; he seems to find it insufferable, if you are also praying.

The power of fasting and prayer extends from here to the ends of the earth. It really does. And the reason for doing them is love. This is the moment when you understand St. Paul: the gifts of prophecy and faith and hope, and all the rest of the gifts, will fall away, and only love will remain.

Fasting means controlling one's appetites. It includes sex as well as food. In old Russia, married people did not cohabit during the six weeks of Lent, nor other times of fasting in the liturgical year. We consider sex an appetite too, so it is quite normal for us to abstain; not because it is sinful or dirty or wrong in any way, but because it is the same as when we abstain from our appetite for food—in order to be more alert to God's voice, to stand, as it were, on tiptoes in order to hear him.

When I have disciplined myself, I can listen to God; whereas when my mind wanders, I cannot. But when I am recollected and directed toward him, things happen. With fasting, it is the heart that begins to open up so you can begin to love; you are capable of going out of yourself toward another.

You are free; nobody tells you that you have to fast, but you decide to fast. The Church invites its people to enter deeply into Lent, and the depth of that entry is measured by the amount of love you have for him whose passion Lent celebrates, reminds us of. It is a question of love.

All asceticism should lead to communion with God. Asceticism—penances and other such practices—done just to show how mortified I am does not lead me anywhere, even if nobody knows about it but myself. That is just self-love. You can beat your body, not eat, and seemingly spend a lot of time in prayer, and yet be adoring yourself. There is always that terrible danger of the golden calf, instead of the Christ of the poor, of Bethlehem, Nazareth, and Golgotha. It is insidious. No wonder he said to the people: "When you fast, wash your face and make your hair shine" (Mt 6: 17)

In the early Church, fasting always meant complete abstinence from all food, and thus being hungry. Fasting of any kind will lead you to doubt and to irritation. I know how it feels when you fast; I gave up cigarettes, and that is exactly how you feel. If you think that your fasting will lead you up to heaven, do not fast.

The moment we get into fasting, we also get into temptation. This is one of the things that takes a little time to understand. The evil one will present you with every reason for not continuing your fast. That is why I turn to Our Lady, the woman who can crush his head with her heel. And I implore her to help me, because I know only too well that I cannot do it by myself.

The first step in any fasting, be it from cigarettes, from cookies, or whatever, is to look at Our Lady, because God has given her a heel that can squash the devil, thus it is good to turn to her and ask her help.

Lent can be very difficult, because it is a time when we face ourselves. And facing ourselves, we discover many things about ourselves—among them our halfhearted service of God. We are like cross-eyed beings, with one eye looking at what we could have, such as food, and the other looking at God, who often seems unattractive compared to it.

When I fast from food, e.g., I have to contemplate it, sort out my relation to it—as I must do with all things, so that I may use them for God's purposes. Food is a wonderful thing because he has given it to me. So are all the things he has given to me. I should worship him who has given them to me, instead of worshiping the things and forgetting God. This is matter for our prayer, as well as our fast.

The fact is, when I begin to fast, when I begin to pray, I say clearly to the devil, "It is obvious that I belong to God, and I want to see God. I am following Jesus Christ." The devil then tempts us by virtue, "You shouldn't fast; you get irritated." Or, "Don't give up smoking; you make everybody miserable. You don't want to make everybody miserable. It's so un-Christian. Why don't you stop? Take a puff." That is how he tempts you. And the answer, of course, is try to fast from irritation.

Nevertheless, prepare yourself that you are going to be attacked, and do not get excited about it. Just say, "Okay, you want to push me around, push me around.

But I'm not going to take that puff of a cigarette, and I'm not going to eat that creampuff full of ice cream and chocolate. I'm not going to do it, that's all there is to it. I love Jesus Christ." So, he retires, goes some place where he can think, and then he comes back and starts again.

One thing I want you to know is that whenever you are moving towards God, the devil will be right behind you saying: "Pssst, there is that other road; pssst, do this, do that." You see how it is. Yet through all this, fasting and prayer will get you over temptation, and then temptation is a beautiful stairway that God permits to happen, just to show us how much he loves us. As Fr. Schmemann writes in *Great Lent*: "A faith which has not overcome doubts and temptations is seldom a real faith. No progress in Christian life is possible without the bitter experience of failure."

Let us take that as a good idea for Lent, because we think failure is terrible. If you fail, you are rejected; if you are rejected you are not loved. Nobody stops to think that failure is a normal thing. Try to understand that when you fail in a struggle with God, you simply see yourself. And that failure leads to a good examen of your own conscience. Failure simply means "get up, start all over again."

Fasting will take you deep. When the apostles told the Lord that they were unable to exorcise devils as he had done, he himself said, "These are exorcised by fasting and prayer." Yes, our fasting can begin to exorcise the many little devils that still live in our hearts, and some of the big ones that hide behind them—Lent is the time to exorcise all of them. Wherever we turn to God, always we come face to face with fasting, prayer, and penance. There is about them a strange fascinating call; they are powerful spiritual weapons.

Fasting simply for the sake of a diet is uninteresting before God. Our fast must be a movement of our soul to liberate itself from the things that hold it wrongly to earthly things. God can use all kinds of fasting.

Fasting is the song of a soul in the process of liberation. It is a door to that dispossession which allows me to give up my will to God. Fasting is the shepherd's crook that leads you and me on the road to the real pilgrimage to God. With that crook, one moves faster. Fasting is the following of Christ, not walking behind him, but running as men and women in love run toward him whom they love.

I am the sister of Jesus Christ, who came to do the will of the Father, and so I desire to do the will of the Father. The will of the Father can be difficult, a heavy burden on my selfishness. By fasting from all my appetites—cigarettes, food, and so forth—I finally develop my will to a strength in which I can shoulder the demands of God that seem to be so heavy on me. And I find that they are not heavy at all, because I have given up that which stood between me and God. This is our consolation. And we discover that one of the biggest by-products of fasting is a new freedom.

Here we have to make very certain that we do not think that we are appeasing God by our fasting. We do not say, "Here are my sins, Lord, and here is my payment or atonement for them." No. We fast to seek the face of our

Father. We fast because heaven is taken by violence, violence to oneself, violence to all those things in us that are not of God. A fast is to remove all that is not of God in us.

I think that is the essence of Lent: when Christ is risen, and we rise with him, we need to be empty of all the junk that should not be there. Then we can lightly follow him, and go where he goes.

Fasting can be a contact with poverty, the beginning of real identification with the poor. If we spend a whole day without food, we would know at the end of that day what it is to be really hungry. And we would know in our body what the poor experience. Somewhere inside our heart, we then begin a contact, a real contact with the have-nots.

Fasting can be identification. But it is a strange thing, because when you fast because of this desire for identification, and you identify with the poor, something changes in you. At some moment you begin to understand what is really happening: it is Christ who is fasting in you, and you are fasting in Christ—because identification with my brother and sister is identification with God. As he has told us, "whatsoever you do to the least of my brethren, you do to me." It is then that you begin to understand a little better what fasting does.

Christ comes into your heart with people. At our house in Edmonton, which has a soup kitchen, there is a big, beautiful mural showing a bread line of men and women. Standing in the midst of the bread line is Christ, with a little halo around him. This is exactly what happens: in our serving the least of our brethren by our fasting, Christ is served. And our hearts are broken open.

We can fast like this wherever we are. People often do not realize that they do not have to leave their homes, their work, the places where they live, to allow the light of the Triune God to shine through their fasting.

For example, even the sick can offer their suffering, part of which might be the need for special diets. If they accept all the realities of their sickness in the spirit of fasting, they are filled with the light of the Holy Spirit. They live then in a luminous, sun-filled place, the rays of which touch thousands of hearts that do not even know they have been touched. But they begin to feel the effects of it.

I used to visit a woman who was crippled with severe arthritis; she ached from top to bottom, and lived in a poor little room. When I looked at her, I would have tears in my eyes. But she would say, "Don't pity me. Rejoice with me. For I am here on my cross that God has given me. I know that just by doing nothing here, just by having pain, I help God and bring people to him. Because we who have pain are on the cross of Jesus Christ, we are one with him. He said, 'If I be lifted up, I will draw all things to myself.' Well, if I am lifted up with him, I can draw people to him. I am like a door to his wounded heart. Here I am, all sick and wounded, and I am a door to him. Isn't that wonderful!"

Those who are sick have something to do for the Lord; their sickness is something to do with the Lord.

My Heart is Ready

No one in his senses would say that we are following a God who is comfortable. No. We are following a crucified Man. A Man who is leading us to crucifixion, the Man who is "the suffering servant" of the Lord. We are following Christ. One of these days each one of us will understand that we can dance on a carpet of pain: the little pain of the emotions, the huge pain of a desert the emotions may produce; the pain of the body, the pain of the mind, the pain of man, and the pain of Christ. All these will come to us. And faith, which cleanses the caverns of the soul, is the healing agent.

In the caverns of our souls there are all kinds of packages that we carefully wrap up: grievances, hostility, neuroses, this and that and another thing. Something that was not joyous. Something that was not laughter. We stuck it there and then forgot about it, but it acts like an irritant. But we must not stick it into any kind of caverns, on any kind of shelves. We must burn it with the fire of the Holy Spirit. We must allow it to disappear.

Fasting conditions the soul and makes even the mind suddenly alert and alive to the fact that it should go deeper—simply, childlike, without tremor. The mind is always facing faith. Faith cannot compromise, and makes one meet God "face to face" in that strange darkness that we travel now in this life. But the mind rebels against this. We must pray and fast to grow in faith. Such conditioning of mind, body, and soul helps us to keep on walking in faith through the darkness of it, through its caverns, its crevices, its peaks and its abysses.

Penance and fasting are part of a cleansing process, a cleansing of the caverns of the soul. There the mind constantly wants to hide a little part of the self that is always warring against faith. The caverns of the soul are full of twists. There is where we hide that will of ours that wars against the will of the Father. There is where we hide our opposition to the laws of Christ, the laws of love. There is where we hide our compromises. They are just at the edge of the shelves in those caverns, so that we can grab at them quickly whenever we want to eliminate faith from our brilliant mind. But faith will not accept any compromise.

Just because we believe, and we surrender, that does not mean that we are not going to be sinful, that we are not going to fall flat on our face. Deep down in us we have resolved that there will be no "maybe". So in the morning we feel moody, and we say, "Lord, I feel moody and I am on my way to breakfast, and I am not going to allow the darkness of my moodiness to darken anybody's mind at any time today." That is the way we go about it.

But we are so astonished when we fall flat on our face that we get mad at God. Or are we mad at ourselves? And that is a sin of pride. Let us expect from ourselves constant weakness. Let us expect sinfulness. Let us expect failure, and let us know that in God alone is our strength, and not add insult to injury, meaning the sin of pride. We are sinners and we fall flat down. Of course we will. Let us pick ourselves up. It is only a hundred times a day!

What is important is the fact that you keep trying, that you have persevered. Notwithstanding the fact that you have fallen, and fallen, and fallen, in humility you realize that you are going to do that until you die. You need not get all hot and bothered, nor say: "Me, such an important person, and I fall down every day? Who do you think I am? I am going to work at not falling down. By myself alone, I am going to work at it. I don't need God. I can do it myself alone."

Do not expect to be a saint without a single blemish; no saint was without a blemish. We acknowledge that we are sinners, but saved sinners; and that with the grace of God, notwithstanding that we fall down a hundred times a day, we are going to persevere. That is all; it is as simple as that.

Do we ever think that Christ prayed a lot? If you read the Gospels you will read that he went into some quiet place and prayed all night sometimes. Then you will read again that he fasted. In fact, he fasted forty days when he was in the desert. It seems that we have forgotten this, and by and large these days we do not fast and we do not pray too much in Lent. Go into your heart; there is the deep stuff inside. Cleanse your soul and your heart of all the junk accumulated through the years: envy, jealousy, a lot of things. Lent is for that.

And as you come out of Lent a great joy will prevail in you and Easter will be a really beautiful time. Beautiful, if your Lent has been true, and one that really cleansed your soul. Do it now, face it. Talk to God and to Our Lady. Talk, so that your room, your soul, may be ready for Christ to walk into.

Book 2

Thoughts in Holy Week

Take Off Your Shoes

The entire Holy Week is a week of tenderness. All through the Gospel, from his birth right up to his death, the Lord exhibits much tenderness, especially in the way he treats the sinner. When the woman taken in adultery is brought to him, (John 8:3-11) Jesus shows great delicacy. It is very delicate to turn your back to a person like that, who is ashamed, write something in the sand, and wait until the last person has left; and then with infinite tenderness and gentleness say, "Has no man condemned you? Neither do I. Go, and sin no more".

When Mary anoints Jesus's feet with ointment (John 12:1-8) and Judas complains, Jesus says, "Leave her alone; she has kept this scent for the day of my burial. You will have your poor with you always; you will not always have me." Tenderness—pity. Not the pity that hurts, the pity that makes the poor feel squeamish inside, not just the passing pity of the mind, but the pity of the heart. Jesus did not break the bruised reed nor quench this kind of flame.

Holy Week comes upon us. We have walked through Lent to come to this week in order to remember. It is painful. Painful because we love God and watch him suffer, yet joyous because we want to cry out our thanks to him. It is our week too in that now we must be crucified. We must go through the suffering he has gone through. That is his great gift to us, that we "make up what is wanting in the suffering of Christ" (Col 1:24). Nothing is really wanting in the suffering of Christ, but he allows us to partake of it if we wish.

It is our week to ask about our love, about how much we love him. It is our week to ask ourselves how much we really follow him. There are thousands of little escapes that we can indulge in, that will make it appear that we are following him when we are not. It is our week to find out if we have kissed a friend in the way Judas kissed God. We can do that hypocritically, to earn human respect.

It is a week of examining ourselves. Not with a sort of a cold, intellectual examination of conscience to count our sins. That is not important; his infinite mercy will cover our sins if only we cry out to him for it. No, it is our week to find out how little we love, or how much. And no matter how much we do love, it is our week to cry out to the Lord to learn to love him more.

It is a fantastic, incredible week, in which we are allowed to see how much God the Father loved, how much God the Son obeyed the Father, and also loved us. It is the week of the Spirit: "I have endowed him with my Spirit" (Mt 12:18).

Each minute, each hour, each day of this week is a pilgrimage interiorized, a journey inward, to meet the Triune God who dwells within us. But also to follow Christ, to follow him from the moment of the changing of the bread and wine, to the stone of agony in the Garden, to the departure of all his disciples—the whole seen like a movie that is constantly before our eyes.

The path is clear. Christ made it; we cannot miss it. There are drops of blood along it, in the sands of time. We must follow them. This is the hour of us breaking all the vases we have in our hearts and spilling upon his feet all the perfumes we ever accumulated throughout our lives. What use have we of perfumes when we have God?

☩   ☩   ☩

This is the week of quiet. That is to say, this week we should have a quiet heart. We are on the threshold of such a miracle that we can repeat the warning: "Take off your shoes, this place is holy."

Let us quieten our hearts again. This is a great week that we are entering. It is the week of total *kenosis*, which in Greek means emptying oneself. When Christ came from heaven at Christmas he emptied himself and became a servant. The theme of servant comes to us again. This is the week of our *kenosis*—what he has done, we should do.

Our hearts become quieter and quieter. And look! Soon there will be a supper, of a kind that has never before been on earth, in which God will give himself to us as food. He who is fed on God is one with God. We are his children and we can do what he can do—with his help. In fact he said, "You will do greater miracles than I." Our faith should rise like a blazing fire during this week, for we know a little of what it is all about. The events of this week shake us and hold us tight in a sense of expectation.

This is the week of Passover, both the first Passover supper that the Lord God asked for in the Old Testament, and the supper of God giving himself to us as food. This is the week of love, of a kind that makes one's head and senses reel. To be fed by God is to be strong. So that by doing what is best for the other person, not by doing what I want, I begin to love.

This is the week of understanding. Although what a foolish word! We do not understand a mystery. No. This is a week of entering without understanding, of putting your head into your heart, so to speak.

At the same time, what we enter into is so extraordinary that we must understand who we are: we are the people who have been salvaged by God. Christ has lifted us to his Father, who had asked him to make us one, to cherish us, to look after us.

This is the week of his joy: "I have longed to eat this Passover with you before I suffer." (Luke 22:15) This is the week of his sorrow. This is the week of his death. We can only prostrate ourselves before a cross and pray a prayer of thanks, the kind of thanks that is torn out of us because it is buried so deep that we do not often bring it forth. This is the hour of thanks.

This is the week of examining our conscience. For it is useless to prostrate, to kneel, or to pray, unless I, too, become a servant of the people that Christ became servant of. When Jesus finished washing the feet of all the apostles, he reminded them that "the Son of Man has not come to be served, but to serve".

We need to set apart a place in our hearts where we are attentive to God, no matter where we are or what we are doing—washing dishes or anything at all. It makes no difference what you happen to be doing, because in your heart you are with your Beloved. Now we enter deeply into that place.

But this is also a week in which I have to serve my brother in whatever capacity I might be needed, because prayer without action is dead. You have to integrate your prayer into your life, preach the Gospel with your actions. Otherwise people will not know that this week is different from any other week that ever was or will be.

☩   ☩   ☩

Without Christ, we can do nothing. I pray that we rely only on God, that we lean on God constantly; then we can restore the world to him. I hope your hearts, like mine, are filled with joy and longing, even though we live in the midst of trials and tribulations.

Just think for a moment how wondrous and beautiful it is to be a Christian, to live in faith. To know—with a knowledge that transcends all intellectual knowledge— that we are now, today, living in the Resurrected Christ. And that we are going rapidly into the heart of the Trinity in a union of love, joy, and happiness that "ear has not heard and eye has not seen," as St. Paul says (1 Cor. 2:9), and mind cannot understand.

What must we do, what must we *be* to reach this ecstasy? We must be what we are, Christians who "work out" hour by hour, day by day, the life of Christ from Bethlehem to Gethsemane to the Resurrection.

All this adds up simply to one little word: we must love. Love, with our burden of emotions, of miseries and doubts, confusions, temptations, because they are the door through which we are going into the *Parousia*, the Second Coming of the Lord. The door is cruciform, true, but it is bearable if we have the faith that is necessary to accept it as lived this very moment, this very day, in the resurrected Christ. He is with us at our computers, our laundry, our meals, our darknesses and our lights, our hard days and our big days. It is in him, with him, and through him that we know that elusive happiness that escapes all those who do not believe in him. With him it is not elusive, or illusive. With him it is real. Happiness is with you, happiness is in you. Love beyond understanding, yet real and touchable, feeds you daily on itself, for the Lord is with us.

Already the light of the Resurrection shines blindingly on this week. We know the darkness is temporary and exists only in time and history—and in our lives, to show us the face of Love that died and resurrected for us, so that we too will enter into that Resurrection.

Let us enter this week with quiet, undistracted hearts, with prayer, with the realization that we are touching Love Incarnate in our hearts, for he has come down to us. Christ has given us his body. He has given us extraordinary powers, while we live the life of love that he called us to.

Palm Sunday

The triumphant ceremony which liturgically opens Holy Week on Palm Sunday of the Lord's Passion teaches us that death leads to life, that the cross is inseparable from God's glory and ours. And that the redemptive sacrifice completes itself only on the day of the Ascension when Christ, conquerer and king, enters heaven to sit at the right hand of the Father.

Our life is intimately bound up with Christ's triumphant mysteries: his death on the Cross, his entombment,

Resurrection, and Ascension. Because of these, you and I will also ascend to heaven and be with God—the Father, Son, and Holy Spirit—in a union of love and joy. Because of these mysteries, we are redeemed; we have faith; we walk in hope; and we have charity, which means that we already possess God who is love.

Our joy in the meaning of these mysteries is reflected in the procession on Palm Sunday, which reminds us of the triumphal entry Jesus made into Jerusalem some days before his death.

Before the procession begins, there is the blessing of the palms. The whole ceremony of their blessing, distribution, and their being carried by the faithful in solemn procession is of ancient origin and was evidently begun by the early Christians.

Palms were and are used in the East, where they are readily available. But here in Combermere, as in my native Russia, we gather pussy willows and cedar branches to carry in place of palms on this day. Whatever is used is blessed, sprinkled with holy water, incensed, and distributed.

Before the procession begins, we read the Gospel of Christ's entry into Jerusalem (John 12:12–15). Once again—how strange—the sound of donkey's hooves are heard. They were heard before Christ was born when Our Lady carried him in her womb on the way to Bethlehem. Now they are heard again.

For his "triumphal" entry into Jerusalem, Christ chose to mount a donkey, and in doing so, without words he again proclaimed himself a servant of the people. "I have come to serve," he said. The donkey itself was a servant. By straddling a donkey to enter Jerusalem, he proclaimed himself a servant.

The prophets had foretold that the holy king so long expected by the Jewish people would use a donkey as his mount. Christ fulfills these prophecies, entering Jerusalem on a meek and humble donkey, with children throwing their cloaks on the road before him.

Like those children, we sing a beautiful antiphon that is a shout of joy, veneration, and welcome: "Hosanna to the son of David, blessed is he who is coming in the name of the Lord!" We become like children again, of such is the kingdom of heaven, as we sing this hymn of the children of Israel.

Then, as if unable to contain ourselves, we burst into a triumphal declaration, sung as before the Ark of God behind the curtains in the inner temple, the Old Testament symbol of the presence of God in the midst of his people. With joy and enthusiasm, in hopes of the day when the entire world will bow to the royalty of Christ, we sing, "Jerusalem! Jerusalem! Lift up your gates and sing! Hosanna in the highest, hosanna to our King!"

Our life can be such a procession; our ordinary, everyday life. What does it matter that instead of palms, we hold tools of all kinds—brooms and dishes and brushes and hammers and books. Every day of our life can be a living "Hosanna" to Christ the King, a march, a triumphal march toward Jerusalem, the City of God, and toward the day of his Second Coming, the Parousia.

During the Mass itself we read the Gospel of Christ's passion. The cries of the crowd, "Crucify him! Crucify him!" are in sharp juxtaposition to the cries of "Hosanna!" during the triumphal entry.

We can remember, as we walk daily in this procession of love and allegiance, that it will lead us inevitably to Golgotha. We should be joyful about that, as we grow in love and faith. For as we grow, an incredible miracle will take place within us by the grace of God: Golgotha, the cross, the tomb will become so very small and easy to accept, even willed, desired, and waited for. Our growing faith and love will center on the Resurrection and the Ascension that guarantees us our heart's desire: oneness with the Beloved.

✠　✠　✠

I was meditating on Palm Sunday, and a thought developed itself in my mind as if on a canvas: that God sent his apostles to find a donkey, and that he rode on it into the big city of Jerusalem.

To the Jews and others in the East the donkey was a beast of burden. People of rank rode the beautiful celebrated Arabian horses. To this day, the Arabian horse is one of the "aristocrats" of the equine world. Kings and other "big shots" travelled on those delicate-looking but strong animals, while ordinary folks used different mounts.

One might have thought that Christ would have entered Jerusalem on one of those prancing Arabian horses, one that lifted its feet so proudly. The donkey is a lowly beast, just an animal to load with whatever you have: merchandise, wood, water. But here comes God, riding on a donkey! To where is he riding? To the city that, for the people of his milieu, was the center of the universe.

Then the strangest thing happened. A humble man on a most humble animal suddenly was surrounded by children who cried, "Hosanna!" People laid their cloaks down on the road for the donkey to step on, and waved palm branches in the air.

Think about that for a moment, in relation to yourself and myself. Do I ride a donkey? Or do I think that the least for me is a Cadillac? I mean this symbolically, of course.

Do I live constantly alert to never open my heart, lest perhaps others think I am not on a beautiful Arabian horse, but on a very humble donkey? If I open my mouth, maybe they will find out I am illiterate. Maybe they will find out I do not know anything. If they find out, maybe they will ridicule me. I do not want to ride on a donkey into those cities of other people's minds. Oh no! I want to make people think that I have a horse—a beautiful, expensive, prancing horse.

So I shut myself up and do not let anyone come near. I am like a porcupine who withdraws under the protection of its sharp quills, bristling against those who come near. "Don't touch me!" is my motto. Because if you touch me you might discover that I am riding a donkey, when I want to be riding through life on a horse.

Why is it that I refuse to be like Our Lord? Why don't I ride into the minds of my fellowmen humbly, on a donkey? Why do I not simply acknowledge that, yes, I come from Galilee as it were (which was not very well thought of in Jesus's day). If I acknowledge the truth about myself, God will come to me and I will lose fear and inhibition, and will appear before everybody as I am.

If we follow in the footsteps of Jesus Christ and are humble enough to ride on a donkey, there is recompense. The joy, the gifts that God showers on those who are willing to ride on a donkey into the minds and hearts of others is beyond computing. We will know an inexpressible joy, the joy of loving our neighbors as ourselves, having loved ourselves first.

It is such a simple formula: a donkey and God; then a donkey, me, and God in me! That is all. Let us let go of our wrappers, our fences, and all those things that stand between us. How will we know each other unless all the fences are down?

Holy Thursday

This whole day is dominated by the memory of the Last Supper, that last supper Christ took with his disciples. In the Holy Thursday Mass, we celebrate the institution of the Holy Eucharist and the sacrament of the Priesthood. Another dominant theme is the commandment that Christ calls his own commandment: to love one another— which the Eucharist is the symbol of and gives us strength to actualize in our lives. This is brought to our attention by the Gospel and the ceremony of washing the feet.

Christ Gives Himself as Food

Before he died, Christ broke a piece of bread and distributed it; he poured some wine and gave it to his apostles and said, "Do this in memory of me". It was in the form of thanksgiving that Christ instituted the memorial of his passion. We call it *Eucharist*, which means thanksgiving. At the consecration, the bread and wine become truly the Body and Blood of Jesus Christ, his offering to the Father. It is Christ whom we receive at Mass. Let your heart be pierced with this tremendous and incredible mystery: that we attend a Mass, and the Lord gives us his Body and Blood in the form of bread and wine—the ordinary food of mankind! Something mysterious and incredible happens. It is incredible because I and God become one!

The very word Communion means union, but what a union! Think of its infinite intimacy—my soul and yours, impenetrated by God himself, who becomes part of us and we part of him! Do you realize the incredible, the glorious love which is behind that giving of himself as food? Of giving himself as a lover does—and he, our God!

Approaching the altar for Communion is the time for us to remember that the Eucharist is a sacrifice as well as a sacrament. It is the sacrifice of the cross in the heart of the Church, which means in your heart, my heart, our hearts, as in our lives, by the adherence of our entire being to the crucified Messiah, who gives us his Passion, his self-offering on the cross, for food. To eat the flesh of the Son of Man, and to drink his blood, is to live the entire mystery of his passion, death, and resurrection.

In a way, it is strange that we use the word "communion" for receiving the Body and Blood of Christ, and that we do not use the words "eating God". For that is what he really said in the Gospel: "unless you eat and drink of my body". We become one with Christ in this eating. Why did he choose this strange form of communication? He reduced himself to the essentials, and the essential for man to live is food. He loved us so much that he communicated his love to us in his becoming food, and me eating it. And in that he and I became one.

In the wilderness God gave his people manna for food. Now the food he gives is himself, and that is the greatest happiness and consolation. Ponder the words: *Now the food he gives is himself.* How utterly incomprehensible. Christians receive food for their journey at Communion. Our spiritual food in this world is the Eucharist.

There is immense joy in possessing the Eucharist, that food from Heaven, the joy of living with our mind lifted to the supernatural world. The deep realization that we have divine life and can live supernaturally, can live the divine life. And the joy of being witnesses in this world to the Risen Christ.

Taking the Eucharist into your heart, you realize dimly, very dimly—for it is a great mystery—what it is. Now, since you and God are one, you can give him to others. The more you receive God, the deeper is the love, and the more open is your heart. And you remember that he who instituted the Eucharist said, "I have come to serve". Prayer and service, or service and prayer, become a natural hunger in our hearts. We communicate with the divine; we are divinized. All things are possible to God.

To participate in this feast of love would be a blasphemy and a terrible lie if we did not love our brethren in truth and in action. He who eats of Christ in the most holy sacrament of the Eucharist must be eaten up, or give himself to be eaten up, by his brethren. I receive Holy Communion: I eat God, and I have the flesh and blood of

Our Lord in me. So I have to share it; I, too, have to be "eaten up" by others. I share with them my being.

As he feeds us in the Eucharist, Christ becomes our strength in our everyday struggles—we are never alone in our battle against evil. We know without him, we can do nothing. Our strength never lies in ourselves, not in our professional competency, not in our intellectual talents, not even in our skills. It lies in the incredible fact that we are one with God, made so by his goodness and love in such an incredible, intimate manner as receiving him, the Lord of Hosts, as food.

Let us thank God for what we have received. Thank him by going forth to do his work of love, beginning with those closest to us. And let us beg God to experience the power of the Sacrament we celebrate, so that as we walk away from the Mass, in which we have all been one in the Lord and each other, we realize that the Holy Spirit has made us adopted sons of God.

Christ teaches us in his parable of a feast (Lk 14:16-24) that the Father wants his house to be filled with those whom he loves so much—really all humanity. Who will be admitted to God's eternal feast? Sinners, the unfortunate, the unwanted—it is to such as these that Jesus sent his apostles. It is for them, too, that the Eucharistic supper is meant—them, and not those who think they have no need of Christ, of God. This is consoling. The Eucharist is not a recompense for the just, but the salvation that God offers to our misery and sinfulness. If we come to it with contrite hearts, we shall be made whole. God has invited us to his banquet of love through sheer mercy.

The Lord constantly and patiently continues to invite us to a wedding feast. This wedding feast begins here on earth in the Church, the assembling place of all those "invited by God". And it is also to heaven's wedding feast that this invitation is extended. For this feast beginning on earth in the Church, will continue in heaven where there will be even greater joy, incredible joy, in the presence of God himself. The Eucharist is the heralding of this banquet.

Let us pause a moment and think of this. As all things that Christ does, it is rooted in love. Our faith is a love affair between God and us, and us and God. Why then are we so slow on the uptake? Why are we so reluctant to respond to this Divine Love? Is it because the sign of our celestial nuptials as it were, the sign of our wedding with Christ, our surrender to him, is cruciform?

The God of Love, who proved his love by dying this painful tragic death on the Cross, is a merciful, tender, compassionate, loving God. But he asks a proof of our love. And that proof lies in the faith and love with which we accept his cross.

Christ Gives Himself in his Priests

Holy Thursday is priesthood day; Jesus Christ brought forth the priesthood when he said, "Do this in remembrance of me". You know, there is a moment in which a human heart pauses and begins to realize, dimly, an infinite mystery that cannot be fathomed, only approached at the edges. Christ ascended to his Father after his Resurrection, but he did not want to leave us orphans, and so we have the priesthood. Christ is with us in our priests; he walks among us in his priests.

There is only one priesthood, that of Christ. But he multiplies himself in the men we call priests so that they can feed us with the Bread of Life—himself! And they can dispense all his sacraments of love to us. So that he can preach through them, heal our souls, and continue to perform greater miracles of grace than those he did in Palestine. Yes, in his immense love, he chose men in whom he could walk, in whom he could forgive sins, who could give us the sacrament of the holy Eucharist, which he said makes for life everlasting.

When a bishop puts his hand on the head of a young man, a middle-aged man, an old man to ordain him, at that moment a fantastic thing happens. Christ enters into him in a totality of entry, the likes of which we cannot even imagine. Now this man is Christ! Christ in him breaks the bread and gives the cup. Christ in him absolves from sin; notice how the priest says, "I absolve you"— "I", meaning Christ. Approach a priest as you would approach Christ, because he has God in him in a very special manner, through the sacrament of Holy Orders.

A priest has the power of healing bodies, of healing souls, of bringing back the prodigal son. He has the power of feeding the hungry: those who haven't bread and those who have, for the Bread that the priest gives assuages the hunger of both poor and rich. The enormity of God's love for us never dawns on us.

Christ loved us so passionately, so foolishly, so beyond all bounds of love that we can experience, that he left us himself in his priests. He takes a sinner, just like ourselves, and through a special anointing and the laying on of hands by a bishop, the man is impenetrated, filled with Jesus Christ. Here is God descending into a sinner, and not only descending, but filling that man with himself. Into these men he has entered, not like milk enters a pitcher, or tea goes into a cup. No. He has become the cup, as well as entered into the cup. Priests really become another Christ. It is the hands of Christ that anoint. It is the lips of Christ that pronounce the words that change the bread and wine into his Body and Blood.

Pray for priests, and thank God that when he ascended to heaven, he left us priests. Let us think about it on Holy Thursday.

As I Have Loved You

Today "the washing of the feet" takes place, in memory of the commandment of Christ to his apostles at the Last Supper. He washed their feet, the Gospel of the day tells us (John 13, 1-15), and said: "If I, then, the Lord and Master, have washed your feet, you should wash each other's feet". We too are to "wash each other's feet"— that is, love unto forgetting ourselves completely, being concerned about each other and those we serve, totally, utterly, completely. "Washing each other's feet" means being the servant of all.

The early Christians astonished everybody by their love for one another. In spite of the diversity of cultures in the Roman Empire, they found a way of loving each other, because love accepts diversity. It could be said about these Christians that they had but one heart and one soul.

At times the early Christians loved one another under terrible conditions. But love is a very difficult thing under all conditions of life, because if it is love, it is selfless; and to love that way Christ wants us to love is cruciform.

We cannot love God unless we love our fellowmen, and we cannot love our fellowmen unless we love God. First we have to make contact with the original community of love, the Holy Trinity. If I make contact with the Holy Trinity, then I am encompassed and embraced in that fire, that flame, that movement that God is—always love, always creation. And then I become on fire, then I can get out of myself, and I can begin to love. I must begin, never expecting it to be done by anybody else; and not trying to be consoled, loved, understood, but to console, to love, to understand.

Are we compassionate? Are we understanding toward one another? Or do we run away from living a Christian life in the world, directly, cruciformly? What is our attitude to the people that we work with in the office, in the school? What about our family? What about loving in a daily, ordinary routine of life? Now that is cruciform.

Christ says, "A new commandment I give you, that you love one another *as I have loved you.* By this shall men know that you are my disciples: that you love one another." How did he love us? It is a very deep question, a question that is only answered by meditating on a crucifix, and realizing that there is a resurrection behind his crucifixion. We are so enveloped in fear, but remember, Jesus Christ said that without him we can do nothing.

Yet it is not enough for me to simply love my neighbor as myself. I must love my neighbor with the heart of Christ. In order to love with the heart of Christ, I have to empty myself of my own heart, so to speak, and acquire his. The process of emptying oneself goes hand in hand with the process of loving.

Who knows what "emptying" was for Christ? We are not God. We can simply surmise a little, with our puny intelligence, what emptying he underwent for love of us. But we know what we have to empty ourselves of—self, the self that so often desires what is the opposite of love, that gets caught in the tinsel, the surrogate, the ersatz.

We have such a tremendous confusion about the word "love" that it is almost unusable in connection with God. What we usually mean is "like". Love takes into its arms the one who is not likeable, the one nobody wants, because of faith.

If you want to empty yourself, try to forget yourself, again and again. And do not get discouraged if you "fail", for with God every moment is the moment of beginning again. I cannot tell you the thousands of ways, in one ordinary day, in a household of any type, the kinds of emptying that have to take place. It is a constant battle until we die.

Love communicates itself to others through your eyes, your smile, your constant, unflagging concern for the other. If you see loneliness in the eyes of a person, and the person is too hurt or too frightened to open the door into that loneliness, cannot give you the key, then go to Christ, who was lonely too, and ask for the key. These are the steps of love, steps that Love will take to help.

As years go by, I pray for only one thing, that I may love my neighbor with the heart of God. I do not fool myself; I know that to love my neighbor with the heart of

God, I have to be empty—even of my own heart, in a sense.

Christ shared our anguish. He shared our pain. Every facet of our sorrows and joys, he himself knows, existentially, because he loved us so passionately. His love is pure and simple, tremendous, incomprehensible, mysterious, beyond the ken of man—a very deep love. Every crucifix shows this.

Christ, so deeply in love with the soul of men, underwent a passion of pain and love unto death. He died slowly, excruciatingly. So anybody who thinks that love has no Siamese twin called "suffering" does not know what love is. Love is inextricably interwoven with suffering.

In order to love, we must empty ourselves of ourself, putting God first, neighbor second, and self third. This must be both inward and outward: it has to come from a deep, flaming faith *inside*, and a love that grows daily *outside*, by the grace of God. We need to die to self until with St. Paul we can say, "I live not, Christ lives in me." Then his heart will love through mine, as he wants it to.

But one cannot empty oneself so thoroughly by oneself. The grace of God is there. He gives us grace, not only grace at moments of our need, but through his sacraments. And of these, the greatest—after Baptism, in which we die with Christ—is the most holy Eucharist. Here the pinnacle of his love is reached.

At Holy Communion, union takes place; in that is our strength to die to self. From there comes our strength for self-emptying, the ability to follow Christ—only there. In him, through him, with him, you will not only be able to do the impossible in a very short time, but you will know *what* to do.

All things must be subordinated to love. It is not the advice we give; it is not the feeding of the hungry and the clothing of the naked; it is not teaching catechism. It is being Christ-bearers. Now, how can we be that when our poor, human clay, filled with emotions, filled with a thousand impulses, tempted by Satan, pummelled by doubts, crying out in our loneliness—how can we love through all misunderstanding, all difficulties, all hostilities, through whatever might come into my path? How can we love that way? We have to undertake the journey inward; we have to go inside of ourselves to meet God who dwells there. We need roots in him. Then, wherever we are, love will spill forth like a sea of fire, because we have made room in us for Christ to go through.

This to me is charity: a fire that is in my heart, in your heart, that nothing can quench, that grows and grows and grows, and washes away self. It is a painful thing, this fire of charity. It burns and it sears, and it plays havoc with the emotions, and it tears the soul apart. And the intelligence cries out to God: "It cannot be that way! You cannot crucify!" Then our eyes fall on a crucifix and I know that when I have crucified all in me that is not God, then my dialogue with another will be perfect.

When you love or I love, we are a mystery. We cannot love the way God wants us to; when we do, it means God loves in us, and that is a mystery. There are always depths into love, depths into self-emptying; they are infinite, because they are always in God's heart.

Good Friday

Today is Love's Day. Today God has shown us how much he loves us. Shown it by dying on the Cross. And thus showing us how we must love him and one another.

Re-read the words of Christ at the Last Supper from the Gospel of St. John. It is good to read it aloud, slowly. See how many times Christ repeated the word "love", how many times he asked us to love one another as he and the Father love one another. How many times did he repeat, oh so gently yet so strongly, "A new commandment I give you: that you love one another". He told us that he was the "way" to the Father, the Father who created us, who so loved us that he sent his beloved Son to redeem us.

Today, celebrating the death of Christ, we in truth are celebrating his awesome proof of love of us. The Resurrection will be the glorious signature on that proof. The Resurrection is proof, too, that it was truly the Second Person of the Most Holy Trinity who for the love of us incarnated himself and died on the cross.

Today is Love's Day. There is sadness and sorrow for his pains. There is a realization of our share in that pain. There is a desire to share in that pain—love always shares! But above all, there is joy beyond expression, joy that mounts in crescendo like the wave of a sea lashed by the winds. Joy and gratitude that surpass human understanding. God loves me! Now the door is open once more to Paradise, and I can, if I love him back, be one with him for eternity.

This is a strange day, a silent day. People across the world are doing the things that they always do, although in certain countries they suspend work on this day. Many have forgotten what this day is all about. Many have barely remembered that Christ is going to be crucified for us today. He allowed himself to be crucified; and "Greater love has no man, than to die for his fellowman". This thought, like the cup of wine and the bread, he leaves for us. For today Christ is in agony; but Christ is in agony always, because we are in agony, and we are his body, the Church.

There are thousands of ways of giving my life to my fellowmen. There is the way of dying to self, facing oneself in the mirror of one's own soul and asking, "How much of my life is spent for me, myself, and I?" and then beginning to change. It will take years maybe, unless God performs a miracle. Very slowly, the person who lived for himself or herself now begins to live for others, in the quiet of their heart. Perhaps it is only known to them and to God, but that is another way of dying. The word for it is "surrender". Not what I want, but what you want, Lord—that is the kind of surrender that God asks of us if we are to give ourselves for and to others.

It is intensely difficult. And it is no use going around talking about God and asking many questions about him. The question that one has to ask is: do I want to follow him or do I not? To surrender to the other is to surrender to Christ: "Whatsoever you do to the least of my brethren you do to me." All around me are my brethren, and my life must be a surrender to them. That is another way to die and fulfil the commandment of God.

He said you must love God your Father with your whole mind, heart, and soul. You must love your neighbor as yourself. It is very difficult to love oneself well. Unless you do it, you cannot possibly love a neighbor, because your first neighbor is you. When you do what you want to do, when you want to do it, at the expense of society or another person, you certainly are not truly loving yourself, ergo you cannot love anybody else.

Moving like a brook moves into a river, one has to love oneself as Christ loved us. He says to his disciples, "By this shall men know you to be my disciples: that you love one another." The hardest thing in the world is to love one another, because we irritate one another so much.

And then he says, "that you love one another *as I have loved you.*" Mind and heart reel before that last sentence. I have to love *as God loves.* Love you, not me. Staggering, isn't it? It is impossible; totally and completely impossible. But he does not stop there. He is the "spendthrift" of love. He says, "Love your enemies" and "Greater love has no man than he lays down his life for the other".

Good Friday is a strange day. Everything is dark—except that at the edge of all the horizons of the world, especially the spiritual world, light rises in strange and beautiful combinations. The sadness of Lent is already turning into joy, because he wanted so much to be crucified for you and me. For by dying he made us alive.

Good Friday is a sad day because his crucifixion was for my sin and yours and those of millions and millions of others. But it is a glad day, because it is the proof of his love.

✠   ✠   ✠

On Good Friday, pain and joy meet in a strange apex, on a fantastic mountain of the Lord. God came and took upon himself the shape of a servant, a slave, for us. He surrendered everything including his body for love of us. He emptied himself.

The great question that stands before us on Good Friday is: are we going to empty ourselves in response to his emptiness? The moment we do, we shall know the joy of Christ! Notwithstanding the pain, the cross, the tomb, if I empty myself because I am in love with God, I shall know joy.

The Eastern Church celebrates Good Friday with flowers and a certain joy. It is as if a person steps outdoors on a sunny day with snow still on the ground, and suddenly through a quiet breeze feels spring! Standing under the cross, my pain in union with his, I feel a joy arising from my heart. Out of the depths of my heart arises the sound, the smell, the joy of spring. Resurrection!

Strange that on this seemingly sorrowful day pain and joy meet. Everybody runs away from the cross, everybody! We do not want it. We like the cross on a table or on a wall; we do not mind it in a church. But when we recall that Christ loved us unto hanging naked on the cross and that we must do likewise, that we must turn the cross around and hang from the other side, we want to break it apart! We think of something else, and so miss the whole point.

God surrendered to his Father's will unto the cross, out of love of the Father and of us. Are we going to bring ourselves to the same surrender, to obey his Father's will? Jesus Christ said, "I am the way to the Father." Surrender, emptying of self, is part of the way of Jesus Christ.

Today joy meets pain, and pain begets joy. God does not speak much today, but in his silence and in his agony he says, "Love me as much as I love you!" It is a solemn day, in which we can descend into the well of our heart and find out how much we love him who loved us so much.

When I see a cross, I do not think about pain or sorrow; I think of fantastic joy. I stand in awe before it. The only thing I feel like doing is to embrace it, to hug it. When you think of the cross, think of joy.

True, you think of pain first; that is obvious, because Christ died on a cross. But have you ever considered that he is the only head of a religious group who undertook to be like we are? We are full of pain, and God shared it all with us.

But it is not the pain that you think of when you see the cross; it is joy. Such a fantastic joy! You think to yourself, "God, the Second Person of the Most Holy Trinity, hung on that cross for me! If I was the only person in this whole world, he would be hanging for me." It turns your head; so you hold onto this cross; you want to kiss it. It is beautiful.

Just think of it. Close your eyes and try to think about it—that Our Lord hung on it three hours for the likes of you and me. It is incredible. But it is the truth. And by doing so he saved us, in the eyes of his Father. Incredible! Absolutely incredible!

The Good Friday liturgy teaches us to realize that we are redeemed. It is not a funeral cortege that we are participating in. It is an act of faith, a tremendous act of faith, a collective one, in the fact that we have been redeemed by Christ through these terrible events of his crucifixion and death that lead to his resurrection and ascension. Our state of soul and mind and heart should be one of openness to the tremendous graces that come to us from the Cross.

The cross dominates the liturgy of Good Friday. Solemnly it is brought in after the reading of the Passion of Christ. Then this cross of Christ is unveiled—slowly, reverently, lovingly—before the eyes of the faithful. One by one these faithful solemnly adore it, using physical gestures that are understandable even to a child. The faithful, from priest to child, prostrate themselves flat on their faces and then kiss the cross.

A passage from St. Paul that I read and reread is this: "For the Jews require a sign, and the Greeks seek after wisdom; but we preach Christ crucified—to the Jews a stumbling block, and to the Greeks foolishness, but to those who are called, both Jews and Greeks, Christ who is the power of God and the wisdom of God. Because the foolishness of God is wiser than men; and the weakness of God is stronger than men." (1 Cor 1: 22-25)

Let us read it this way: some people require a sign; many seek after wisdom. But we Christians are to preach Christ crucified to all. It is considered to be absolute idiocy to die on a cross. Why? None of us, whoever we are, want to accept today that the foolishness of God is wiser than men, and the weakness of God is stronger than men. For when we have human wisdom, with the accent on "human", then Jesus Christ's crucifixion is indeed foolishness.

Why accept the foolishness of God? Why would I want to accept weakness, when I am supposed to be strong, when I am supposed to stand on my own two feet, when I am supposed to look the world in the eye and be a "big shot"? It contradicts everything.

Christ, in his suffering, was a man about whom the scriptures say, "so disfigured did he look that he seemed no longer human" (Isaiah 52:14). Nothing about him was beautiful, nothing! He was whipped with horrible whips. He was bleeding all over the place. He fell on the way to Golgotha, with his robes torn and his wounds filled with dust. He was crucified naked. There was nothing about him that was admirable or good looking or anything like that. That was our God. If there was any weakness to be shown, that was it!

This supposedly great God, who could have called upon all heaven to destroy those characters who were killing him—he did not do any of those things! Scripture links him to a lamb led to the slaughter. Well, what is weaker than a lamb in the hands of men who are going to kill him? Yet, we are horrified to detect signs of weakness in ourselves, and we are more horrified if somebody else points them out to us.

People always expect that when they connect with Christ, everything is going to be alright! It begins to be everything all wrong! You see, when you follow Christ, the first thing that you do is take a terrible risk, to have all the doubts assail you, the devils and his nephews and so forth, and yourself and your emotions and the struggle between your desire to be who you want to be, and your surrender to God. When you join Christ, you really join a battle with yourself. Heaven is taken by violence — violence to oneself!

What is it all about? It is about faith, as usual. Because this happened to him, such things happen to us. And this demands, imperatively, simply, naturally, easily that we believe in the resurrection of the dead. If we believe in God, we believe in the resurrection of the dead, you and I. How, when, which way? Who cares? Why exercise our febrile and fertile brain over mysteries? That is not what mysteries are for. Mysteries are to believe in. What we know is that Christ is with us now and forever, every moment, every minute, every second.

Holy Saturday

Today is a great, holy, and joyful day. We have finished Lent, which is strenuous, but do not yet end our Lenten practices during the day. But the heart is ready. Something very deep in us says, "You have been saved. You have been redeemed. Christ loves you. And in a little while, he will be here and you shall see his face."

Today Christ is in the tomb. God has died for you and for me, for every murderer, for every saint, for everybody who has or ever will walk the earth. There is not a single person for whom he has not died. Doesn't that make you feel that you are loved?

Jesus Christ was born in a borrowed cave and laid in a tomb that did not belong to his family. At this moment, liturgically, he lies wrapped up in somebody else's shroud. He was naked on that cross, he had no loincloth. He was naked when he was born, even as you and I, and he was naked when he died, as you and I will be. I pray that we become naked of our own will, remembering that we are brothers and sisters of Christ, and that we do what Christ did. As he said, "I have come to do the will of my Father. Not my will, but the Father's."

We can contemplate that he died for us. And somewhere deep within us, joy rises like the sun rises early in the morning. But it is still dark, and the darkness is I, looking at myself. The darkness is also my sorrow that he had to die for me. But the joy is that he did! Now all is well. Now I walk in the mercy of God. We live in his mercy, and his forgiveness. He was born to die and resurrect, so that we might be saved. He lies in the tomb for love of you and me.

This day of Christ's burial a sort of desolation can seem to creep in, as we behold his tomb. But at the same time, if we see deeply enough into it, we will see that already the light of the resurrection is so vivid that it lights that tomb.

Once I said to Christ, "You were in a tomb, but if you want a comfortable tomb, here is my heart." I like him to be comfortable in my heart. I can make this "tomb" into a nice, comfortable womb, if I love. Let us make it comfortable for him. Let us all love together, because unless we love, there will be no resurrection of Christ in us, and we will not resurrect in him. Without love, we really are dead, the "living dead". Who wants to be a living dead? Nobody.

So, while he "sleeps", as the scriptures say, let us take a deep breath and say to him, "You died for us. Teach us how to love one another, because you died for that, didn't you?" For on love we shall be judged.

To love is to be crucified. That is a fantastic thing about God: when you are ready for the nails, suddenly, there are no nails. There is nothing but joy. So let us love one another.

✠ ✠ ✠

It came to me that if I wrap myself up in Christ's shroud and meditate on his death, I become more alive! So I wanted to nestle into that shroud. I wanted it to cover me. I wanted to feel its warmth, its life, because I think the shroud of God was full of life. For he rose and the shroud was left behind.

I enter into that shroud or cover myself with it, and the Lord gives me the grace to meditate on his death. To meditate on the death of God is to meditate on the words, "Greater love has no man than he lays down his life for his brethren." As you meditate on it, you really begin to understand Christ's love. Can you direct your heart to this love, and allow the shroud to cover you? The infinite, incomprehensible, incredible God became man and shrouded himself with death.

It entered my heart just how precious we are. Stop and think: the vilest sinner, the greatest saint, and everybody in between is infinitely precious. What else could they be, for Christ became mortal by becoming man, wrapped himself in a shroud, out of love for you and me! Not just love of "humanity", but of each one of us individually. So when you look at the shroud, what else can you have but hope?

This hope becomes a reality because he did resurrect. His resurrection is not a fairy tale, nor a fable. It is the greatest reality in the whole world! We move in that resurrection. When you come close to a shroud, a cross, a tomb, you see it all vanish before your eyes, because the light of the resurrection is dazzling bright.

It holds you tight and lifts you up. Now our blind eyes can see and our deaf ears can hear. It seems so beautiful, I felt like dancing. My meditation was on a shroud, and I am still filled with the joy of it. The shroud enveloped the world and became the flag of the resurrection!

In the Creed we say Christ "descended into hell and on the third day rose again". While in the tomb, Christ was active, raising from "hell" (meaning Hades, the place of the dead) all the just who had lived and died up to the moment of his resurrection.

The icon of Christ's "Descent into Hades", depicted on the cover of this book, portrays the risen Christ vigorously drawing Adam and Eve out of their tombs, grasping them by their wrists. This symbolizes the fact that of their own they have no power to rise from death; their hands cannot grasp Christ's. Adam and Eve symbolize all the just who died prior to the death of our Savior. Christ is shown amid rocks split open (Mt 27: 51–53), allowing the dead to come forth. He stands on the broken gates of hell, rescuing mankind.

The meaning of this icon can be found in an "Ancient Homily on Holy Saturday", from the Office of Readings for Holy Saturday. This reading gives a word dimension to what the icon of Christ's Descent into Hades expresses in art—the whole mystery of our redemption:

Something strange is happening—there is a great silence on earth today, a great silence and stillness. The whole earth keeps silence because the King is asleep. The earth trembled and is still because God has fallen asleep in the flesh and he has raised up all who have slept ever since the world began. God has died in the flesh and hell trembles with fear.

He has gone to search for our first parent, as for a lost sheep. Greatly desiring to visit those who live in darkness and in the shadow of death, he has gone to free from sorrow the captives Adam and Eve, he who is both God and the son of Eve. The Lord approached them bearing the cross, the weapon that had won him the victory. At the sight of him, Adam, the first man he had created, struck his breast in terror....

Christ took him by the hand and raised him up, saying: "Awake, O sleeper, and rise from the dead; and Christ will give you light."

I am your God, who for your sake have become your son. Out of love for you and for your descendants I now by my own authority command all who are held in bondage to come forth, all who are in darkness to be enlightened, all who are sleeping to arise. I order you, O sleeper, to awake. I did not create you to be held a prisoner in hell. Rise from the dead, for I am the life of the dead. Rise up, work of my hands, you who were created in my image. Rise, let us leave this place, for you are in me and I am in you; together we form only one person and we cannot be separated.

For your sake I, your God, became your son; I, the Lord, took the form of a slave; I, whose home is above the heavens, descended to the earth and beneath the earth. For the sake of you, who left a garden, I was betrayed in a garden, ... and I was crucified in a garden.

See on my face the spittle I received in order to restore to you the life I once breathed into you. See there the marks of the blows I received in order to refashion your warped nature in my image. On my back see the marks of the scourging I endured to remove the burden of sin that weighs upon your back. See my hands, nailed firmly to a tree, for you who once wickedly stretched out your hand to a tree.

I slept on the cross and a sword pierced my side for you who slept in paradise and brought forth Eve from your side. My side has healed the pain in yours. My sleep will rouse you from your sleep in hell. The sword that pierced me has sheathed the sword that was turned against you.

Rise, let us leave this place. The enemy led you out of the earthly paradise. I will not restore you to that paradise, but I will enthrone you in heaven. I forbade you the tree that was only a symbol of life, but see, I who am life itself am now one with you... The throne formed by cherubim awaits you, its bearers swift and eager. The bridal chamber is adorned, the banquet is ready, the eternal dwelling places are prepared, the treasure houses of all good things lie open. The kingdom of heaven has been prepared for you from all eternity.[1]

At midnight in the Holy Saturday liturgy the incredible fact of Christ's resurrection will be proclaimed in song, and celebrated in the Eucharist. And we will know that God is alive.

No one knows at what hour his resurrection took place. And who cares? Jesus Christ rose from the dead and the whole world was changed; history was changed; everything was changed. In our hearts we hear a radiant love song, if we have ears to hear.

This night is the night of nights. The night of nights! It should be a night of such a profound love for one another that we know—through the tremendous mystery of faith, which one knows with the heart and with the soul— that each one I love *is* the Lord. Christ meets Christ. This tremendous surge of love should fill us, so that at least one night in all the year we might try to love him and one another as he loves us.

---

1   *The Liturgy of the Hours, Vol. II, Lenten Season, Easter Season.* New York: Catholic Book Publishing Co., 1976.

Book 3

The Easter Season

The Feast of Feasts!

Easter—the resurrection of Christ! The feast of feasts! The final proof of Christ's divinity! Easter—the first feast of the early Church, around which all the other feasts grew like stars around the sun.

We celebrate Christ's resurrection as something absolutely, fantastically beautiful that has happened, and is still happening. The fact that there *is* an Easter is something to be grateful for. It is such a happy feast. What can be more beautiful than this passage from death to life, real life? Now death has become a passage. A passage to what, to where, to whom? It is the passage of you to God and me to God. You walk into it and there at the end is Christ and Our Lady, the life that lasts forever and that is lived with God and his blessed Mother. Christ's resurrection is the most joyous feast in the calendar of the Church, the one in which everything comes together. It is the greatest feast.

As you approach the church for the Vigil Mass announcing Christ's resurrection, you will see preparations for a new fire. The fire is usually lit with a flint as it was in the old days. Ideally, the new fire is a large bonfire lit in the parking lot or other outdoor gathering place. It should be outside of the church on a dark night, because this bonfire celebrates, cries out: "Light! Out of the darkness of the tomb came Light! See! Come here, all you who were mourning. Come, all you who did not believe in God. Come, all you who never were told about God. Come and warm your hands at the fire!" The Light of Christ! This fire is the symbol of light, of warmth, the symbol of the heart of Christ and the love of Christ.

People gather around the fire, which the priest blesses. And from this fire is lit the Easter candle.

Much of the incredible love of God for us is expressed in symbols. To express that Christ is "the beginning and the end", the Paschal candle is inscribed with the letter Alpha (A), the beginning of the Greek alphabet, and Omega (Ω), the last letter, with a cross in between. The four corners of the cross are marked with the numerals of the current year.

Look at this blessed candle carefully, because it is an important symbol. It will meet you at your baptism; it will escort you at your funeral when you are put into the earth to resurrect to a greater light—that of Jesus Christ! After the Vigil Mass of Christ's Resurrection, it will burn at the altar until Pentecost when the Holy Spirit is sent to us.

Deep down in all our hearts we walk in darkness these days. For example, people come from big cities and tell us how frightening it is to walk the streets at night. There are lights, plenty of lights, but yet it is dark! In so many places people walk in fear for their lives, even in illuminated thoroughfares. A friend of ours in Washington D.C. was walking from her job at four o'clock in the afternoon, when she was assaulted by a mugger who took her purse. That was four o'clock in the afternoon, but it was dark. In a sense the darkness of noon is covering the earth today.

Have you lit the Christ candle in your heart? With it, you walk in light. The answer to our darkness of today is faith, which we interiorize by prayer. Faith is that candle of Christ that we allow to burn in our hearts so as to walk by its light. But we are human—small, frightened. We must pray; inwardly we must pray constantly to the Lord to give us faith. That is one gift that the Lord never refuses. Keep that Easter candle trimmed in your heart. Let us all keep ours lit, so that no matter how dark the environment, we have faith, we have light.

After the lighting of the Paschal candle, the priest and people walk in procession from the outdoor fire into the church, which is still in darkness. The priest or deacon holds the candle high. He sings: "Christ our light!" and we all answer: "Thanks be to God!" All the people now light their candles from the Christ candle, and the procession moves on into a dark church, filling it with the light of everybody's candles, including Christ's. A second and third time the priest or deacon chants, "Christ our Light!" as the people fill the church, and when all are in place, the candle is placed on its stand and honored by incensing it.

This is one of the moments I cherish so much every year, one of the most moving ceremonies of our liturgical year. In my Russian culture, during the whole Paschal season people kissed this candle, considering it as Christ, just as Christ is in icons. As Christ is in the Word. And as Christ is uniquely in the Holy Eucharist. As Christ is in you and me. All this we acknowledge as we kiss the Paschal candle.

Yes, Easter is the apex of feasts, the feast of all feasts—Christ is risen! How can I express the immensity of this feast? It is eternal—it picks you up and drops you into eternity.

On this day of Christ's resurrection, *we* resurrect; and so we can grow in love of one another. Love dwells with us. We are to love one another as Christ has commanded:

"Love one another as I have loved you." We ordinary human beings are lifted up in some fantastic, incredible, incomprehensible, mysterious way in this feast so that we may do so.

God loves me. He loves me when I am good and when I am not so good, because he loves sinners. He forgives them too. His mercy is infinite and so is his love, his goodness, his forgiveness. My hand nestles quite easily in the immense hand of God and I shiver with delight.

Christ is risen! Let us love one another as Christ loved us. Then we are clothed in the shining garments of one who is baptized, one whose garments shine from far away and even through the night. Then we become a light to our neighbor's feet.

☩   ☩   ☩

In these our strange and tragic times, we can easily see that all around us, creeping as a sort of a slow fog, comes fear, fear and despondency and depression. And who is going to enter into that strange world that is right in front of us? We look at the inhumanity of man to man, whole countries going hungry, so that if no help comes to them they will perish, especially the children. In many countries the tremendous chasm between poverty and riches is so visible you can touch it. Governments think the way to save money is to cut off aid for the sick, aid for the poor. Every government is looking around to see if they can cut a million or two, and it seems that their faces are directed to those who have not got much. The motto seems to be "I look out for myself".

That sort of situation begets despair. What are you going to do against this, except live hope? Maybe just a remnant of hope has not died in the hearts of men today. But before you can give hope, you have to live faith. People are bewildered; they do not know where to go. As in the scripture, "They shall call to you and say that I am here and I am there and I am elsewhere. Do not believe them." (Mt 24: 23)

What can we do? What should every Christian do? We have before our eyes the resurrection of Jesus Christ. That is our hope, isn't it? That is the antidote that upsets the poison of fear and despair. The resurrection brings light, and deeds that are done in darkness cannot be done in the brilliant light of the resurrection.

The graces of God have been given to each of us to preach the Gospel with our life, no matter what the price, so as to offset despair. When a person is in despair, we can walk into their midst unafraid, because we are cruciform, walking under the sign of the cross that changes into the sign of light—the resurrection. We are the resurrection; we are the Gospel; we are what Christ taught us to be—at least we try. If in their moment of despair a person meets someone who believes, loves, and hopes, then they begin to believe, to love, and to hope.

We live at the end of an era and the beginning of another. They can only be bridged by love, by faith, by hope. This is the hour of opening my heart to your heart, of opening your heart to my heart. This is the hour of unity.

This is you and I walking our own Stations of the Cross that God has given us. The price is pain. The price is falling in the dark on various roads that we travel, sometimes to fall in the dust, sometimes in the mud of the road. Yet always knowing that this road leads to a light that can transform this world, if we allow it to penetrate through us.

Ask yourself, "Am I a Christian in the reality of a situation?" True, you are a Christian because you are baptized, but is it enough simply to be baptized? You have to implement your baptism—make it alive and pulsating and tremendous.

You and I were born and baptized to become ambassadors of God. An ambassador is one who is sent, an apostle of the Lord. All of us are his apostles. Do we act as one who is sent to preach the Good News, to bring hope where there is despair, to bring love where there is hate, to bring faith where there is discouragement? The time is now for us to *be* the Gospel.

The Resurrection of Christ bought us the new life which we received on the day of our baptism. We say that death is no more—which does not mean that physical death has been abolished; it will come to each one of us. But Jesus Christ changed the very nature of death, made it a Passover into the kingdom of God. This is the door we just walk through and we are united with God. In the Byzantine Easter liturgies, we say over and over that Christ has "trampled death by his death". He made us partakers of his resurrection. During Easter time we say, "Christ is risen and no one dead remains in the grave." Christ's Passover from death to life is the end of all that is old, and the beginning of all that is new, a passage from this world into the kingdom of heaven revealed by Christ.

We can just dimly realize what is meant when we say, "in baptism we died with Christ, and we shall resurrect with him" (Rom 6:8). To me it means very simply that having imitated his death, we will be able to imitate his resurrection. If we have truly accepted what our baptism means, we have been crucified with him, we have really died with him; and we will rise with him.

We renew our baptismal vows during the Easter liturgy. What does it mean to renew them? It means to walk in the footsteps of Christ. It means to imitate him. It means to do so without compromise. It means to change the world, and to turn its face to Christ. Why is the world not turned to Christ? Why, after the Incarnation, are people running after everything except God? What are they all running around for? As if they were in ever-faster, whirling dances, with their hands out, crying, "Where is the answer that I am looking for?" And finding out, at the end, that they have not found the answer, and falling down exhausted by the whirlwind of their pursuits, with or without drugs.

All this happens simply because we who are Christians, who really believe in Christ, have not become the imitators of him. So no one has caught who he is, what he is. We have not quite really understood; or if we have understood, we have not the guts to imitate him. That is why the world is the way it is.

Are we new this Easter? This Easter that has been given to us? Once again, we have remembered the life and death of Jesus Christ. Once again, we have witnessed his resurrection as spoken to us by his apostles and by the witnesses. What are we going to do this Easter?

We are going to greet each other in his name; we are going to rejoice; we are going to sing. But what of Monday; what of Tuesday; what of Wednesday? And all the Mondays and Tuesdays and Wednesdays till the next Easter? Are we going to live as if we really died with Christ and resurrected with Christ in our baptism? Or are we going to put aside our baptismal vows, so to speak, and wrap them up in a nice baptismal robe till next Easter? Which will it be?

For we have a fantastic decision to make: to accept the responsibility to show Christ to my brother, to be involved, to be a person of service, like Christ who washed his disciples' feet. Or to drop the involvement and the responsibility, and let our hands flop at our sides, look in a thousand mirrors of our own making, seeing only ourselves, forgetting that we are the image of God. Which is it going to be?

Christ's Resurrection is the earth in which the seed of faith can grow. His Resurrection, when we look at it, opens the tombs of our hearts. Can you hear the stone of doubts, of fears, of expectation, of loneliness, roll away from your heart as it rolled away from his tomb? You and I are transfigured and resurrected, too, in an inner resurrection that is like a fire, like an exploding sunrise.

The resurrection of the Lord from the dead is a call for resurrection—yours, mine, and everybody's—from that apathetic Christianity that exists among us today. If we have given ourselves to Jesus Christ, we can give him to others who are in quest of God, the sea of people who move from one place to another seeking, not knowing what they seek. People who hunger for him today, but are confused by a thousand voices in a meaningless sea without any shores, with waves that chase each other without getting anywhere. We can assuage their hunger because we have been baptized in the death and resurrection of Our Lord. We can give them Jesus Christ if we are in love with him, the Christ who is in our midst.

Christ's Ascension

Jesus Christ ascends to his Father, and has power over heaven and earth, you and me. It is a joy to know that we are in his hands. And we know that as he mounts, so shall we; we too will ascend.

God the Father calls his beloved children to his most sacred and hidden abode, symbolized by the clouds which enveloped Jesus at his Ascension. He is a loving Father whose most earnest desire is to draw all his children as close as possible to himself. The words of Jesus in the Gospel express the Father's will: "Father, I desire that they may be with me where I am." And he is with the Father.

What is the Ascension? Is it a movement to that infinity that we call "the cosmos", Paradise? That is not too important. The important thing is that it is to the heart of the Trinity. The Ascension is an arising, a moving upward—beautiful, joyful. Behind it is the Spirit, the Spirit which we receive in Confirmation. He shows us how to live in order to ascend with Christ, providing we open our hearts again and again to his influence.

In the second reading for this feast, St. Paul says, "May the God of our Lord Jesus Christ, the Father of glory, give you a Spirit of wisdom and perception of what is revealed to bring you to full knowledge of him." (Eph. 1:17-18) "The full knowledge of him"—now Christ has power over everything, for that is what his Ascension means. He is king, he is glorified, he is at the right hand of the Father. And as the song says, "He's got the whole world in his hands." That is exactly what is happening: all of us are in there in the hand of Jesus Christ.

We come to the essence: the Father loved us so much that he sent his Son, Christ God, the Second Person of the Most Holy Trinity, who becomes man for love of us. This love cascades constantly over all of us since we were created, like a million Niagaras. Picture that immense Niagara falling over us, with all the graces and the love of Father, Son, and Holy Spirit. Then realize that this love is in a hand, where the world, the cosmos, rests—a hand pierced with a nail.

Who can be afraid of God when he knows that he is held in the hand of Jesus Christ, in the hand of mercy? I am in the pierced hand of the Lord!

In the Gospel for the day (Luke 24:46-53) Jesus says to his disciples:

"So you see how it is written that the Christ would suffer and on the third day rise from the dead, and that in his name repentance for the forgiveness of sins would be preached to all nations, beginning from Jerusalem." Then he took them out as far as the outskirts of Bethany, and lifting up his hands he blessed them. Now as he blessed them, he withdrew from them, and was carried up to heaven. They worshiped him

and went back to Jerusalem full of joy; and were continually in the temple praising God.

"Repentance for the forgiveness of sins would be preached to all nations." We all are on this immense hand that was pierced with a nail, and "repentance will be preached from Jerusalem". Repentance leads to forgiveness, and forgiveness leads to joy, the absence of fear, the termination of guilt—because the Lord is merciful. How else could he be? Two hands pierced by nails, two feet pierced by nails, a side that has been transfixed with a lance—and we worry about our repentance? We go to confession and yet we say, "I don't feel that I am cleansed." From what? If I repent, if I simply say, "Sorry, Lord," he has already forgiven. And then you are as clean as a little newborn baby! God has forgotten your sin. Let us rejoice, so that we will ascend!

The Ascension is my glory, and in it is a promise: Christ went up, and I shall go up. In my mind, I do not think of being "up there" as some place. I have a sense that I exist in Christ, and that when death comes it will be like an explosion, and then I shall know that I exist within him.

We need to remember that the ages between the Ascension and the Last Day are used properly only if they prepare the world for Christ's final coming. There must be a goal in this life, and the goal is Jesus Christ. And what can be greater than the Second Coming? You are going to be alive forever in the One who loves you, the one you have been seeking. I pray, "On your Ascension day, Lord, give me an ascending heart."

How do we rise with Christ? What is the essential act of rising? Love—we come to that little word. Always the essence is *love*. We too will ascend, but not alone—we take with us all those that the fire of our love and our dedication will lift with us.

Book 4

Pentecost: The Holy Spirit

Who is the Spirit?

On Pentecost day, God's mercy and love came in the shape of tongues of fire and hovered over the heads of his apostles, filling them with unending joy and the gifts of the Holy Spirit. Who is this Holy Spirit? The Advocate, the Consoler, the Father of the Poor, the third Person of the Most Holy Trinity.

Pause for a minute. Try to shut out all the noises within and outside of you. Try with his grace to catch a tiny glimpse of the intensity of the love of the Father for the Son and of the Son for the Father. So awesome, incomprehensible, and passionate is the love of the Father and the Son for one another that it becomes visible, as it were, and begets the Third Person of the Most Holy Trinity, the Spirit of Fire, the Spirit of Love.

Listen with your hearts and your souls. Listen with an ear attuned, with expectation, desire, and love, and you will hear the coming of the wind of the Holy Spirit. This wind is mightier than any tornado. He comes with a speed that cannot be measured. Yet he is as gentle as the evening breeze, swift, immense, harmless to nature and to man. Not only is he not harmful, his passage brings light and warmth, peace and wisdom. He is bringing fortitude, long-suffering, charity, faith, and hope—all the gifts and virtues that are his to give.

Why does he come again? In Confirmation has he not made you once and for all a lover of Christ? Has he not prepared you already for all of the trials to come, even to martyrdom?

Yes, he has done that. But like God the Father and God the Son, the Holy Spirit knows our weaknesses. So, sent by the Father through the Son, he comes every moment of our lives to help us to become saints, lovers of God.

He also comes to console us. Who is there among us who does not need his consolation and fortitude to face another day with love and not with selfishness? The Holy Spirit helps us to love.

The Father of the Poor comes to make us rich. When we speak about our poverty, we speak theologically. While we creatures of God are poor because we have nothing of our own, at the same time we are rich because we are created in the image and likeness of God. Above all, we are rich because God loves us. Thus, we are both poor and rich, but we certainly need the Father of the Poor to make us see how rich we are.

At Pentecost he comes: the Advocate, the Consoler, the Enlightener, the Gift and Virtue Giver, the Father of the Poor. And remember that in the life of a Christian, every day is a Pentecost. Every day the mighty Wind comes, if only we call upon him. Every day the tongues of flame descend upon us, if we realize our need for them and desire them with a great desire.

The Fire and the Wind

We should approach Pentecost not only with awe, but with infinite gratitude. Let us see why. Pentecost is an entry into the fire of the Holy Spirit. It is an entry into the Wind. There is the wind, and there is fire.

Now, wind has a way of its own. When it is of a certain strength it cleanses things. It cleans the roads, gets the leaves off the lawn. It also refreshes and relaxes. The wind has a way of lifting one up. I can just imagine that the wind that came from God at Pentecost took the mind, the soul, the heart, the person of the apostles and simply lifted them up. Then the fire illuminates, and warms, and makes things clear. The fire makes clear what was unclear, like when you bring a lamp into a dark room.

The Fire and the Wind. The lifting up of man to God. And the descent of God into the heart of man, the descent of the Third Person of the Most Holy Trinity.

On each of us, the fire of the Holy Spirit acted in an invisible way at our Confirmation. And we have the Fire and the Wind with us always. We have to remember that in each one of us, at all times, the Fire and the Wind are there.

We have been baptized in water and the Spirit, and we have been confirmed by those to whom God has given the power of bringing that Spirit—but we forget those things. We do not reaffirm in our own heart, as we grow older, that this has happened to us; and because this is so, we let things ride. Let us lift our hearts, our minds in prayer so that the world unplugs its ears and listens to the Wind, that the human heart opens itself and sees the Fire. Let us pray for that, because it is so important.

Today the Church celebrates the constant action of the Lord Jesus. In the upper room, in signs of wind and fire, speaking in tongues and marvelling crowds, the breath of the Spirit is upon us.

On this feast of Fire and Wind, pray to God to cleanse our hearts, our souls, our minds of all the things that are not his. Cry out to God and ask him to send the fire to burn all things in you and me that impede his coming into our souls. Pentecost is the baptism of the Spirit but also the "baptism of fire" of love.

It is so important to know that "There are a variety of gifts but only one Spirit" (1Cor 12: 4). To understand this is to understand who we are and where we are going. We are children of Love, of the Fire and the Wind; God has sent this fire to renew the earth, and this fire does not only come at a certain moment in time. It comes every moment, at all times, provided you and I understand who the Father, the Son and the Holy Spirit are, so that we can give to others the gifts that we have received.

Do we allow ourselves to be caught up in that Wind that makes all things new, that renews the face of the earth and should renew the face of our souls? Or are we like ostriches hiding our heads in the sand of old habits, old ways? Stubbornly refusing to be caught by the Wind of the Spirit that tries to sweep us clean to show beauty to the world once more?

It is so easy to hide from the Wind. It is easy to let it pass by without being caught up by it. It is easy to stay put, behind closed doors and windows, pleading that winds are drafty, that they may sweep corners of our souls that we have not looked at for many years. It is so easy to plead that we are too set in our ways, too tired to allow ourselves to be "spring-cleaned" by the Wind of the Holy Spirit.

For the fresh air that the Wind brings is rarified. It demands of us tremendous efforts. It pleads and asks for a re-examination of mind, soul, and heart that frightens us, because instinctively we know that this will lead us to a change, a complete change in our lives.

If we accept being renewed and cleansed by the Wind, we will have to face without compromise the teachings of the Gospel. We will hear the healing, yet demanding, words of God that allow little compromise and no place to hide.

We will begin to understand that our faith is a love affair between God, who loved us first, and ourselves, whom he asks to love him back. We will realize that we must face the fact, the inescapable fact, with all its tremendous communal, national, and international implications, that we are "our brother's keeper". We will have to cleanse our hearts of idolatry, for we worship many things, many idols, like status, comfort, power and wealth.

We will look deeply into the eyes of Christ. And once we have done that, we will never be the same.

Gifts of the Spirit

All the gifts of the Holy Spirit are sent to us by the Father, the gentle, loving Father who loves us beyond measure. At the moment of Pentecost, the Trinity should be the very essence of our thoughts, for the Father so loved us that he sent the Son, and the Son, when he went back to the Father, sent us the Spirit so that we should remember what he said. Jesus Christ came to do the will of the Father. And I am Christ's sister, and you are his brothers and sisters, and we exist to do the will of the Father, even as Jesus Christ did.

But because we are human and so terribly weak, and because above all we want to put away from us the pain that goes into incarnating Jesus Christ in our body—that is to say, his law of love—the Holy Spirit comes. The Wind and the Fire lift us up.

Now why did the Holy Spirit come? Why would the Wind and the Fire lift us up? Because he changes us into the bride of Christ.

There is a tremendous love affair going on, of which the Holy Spirit is the witness. For what were we created? For a love affair with God! For a oneness with God that nothing can break. For this the Holy Spirit has come. For this, the symbol of the Wind is lifting us up. For this, the symbol of Fire cleanses us and makes our soul afire with love.

St. Paul says, "One Spirit was given to us all to drink" (1 Cor 12:13). The Spirit fills us with that drink from which no one thirsts, if he really cleanses his soul and mind and heart. And to be always filled is to give it to others; that which I drink I must give to others. I am so filled to the brim that I cannot keep it to myself, I have to give it away. I become, in a manner of speaking, a fountain, for I have drunk the Lord and now anyone can drink of me. The Holy Spirit comes to put fire on earth so that it may be lighted; so that we might be united. What are the gifts of the Holy Spirit for? To love God and love one another.

In the Gospel of John (20:19-23) we read:

In the evening of that same day, the first day of the week, the doors were closed in the room where the disciples were, for fear of the Jews. Jesus came and stood amongst them. He said to them, "Peace be with you!" and showed them his hands and his side. The disciples were filled with joy when they saw the Lord, and he said to them again, "Peace be with you! As the Father sends me, so I am sending you."

Here Christ says something fantastic that should send shivers down our spines, that we should hold in our hearts and never let go: "As the Father sends me, so I am sending you." He said it to the apostles, but what he says is meant for you and me. And it means that we have to go.

Whoever we are, old or young, rich or poor—what is our real vocation? Whatever other vocations God might send us, the very essential vocation of the Christian is apostolic. An apostle is one who is sent by someone bigger than himself. That is you and me. It does not matter if we have any education. Nothing matters, because he has sent us, and he has said, "Open your mouth and I will speak". On the feast of Pentecost the Holy Spirit, Wind and Fire, came to teach us what to say. We must have no worries, no inferiority complexes, because we are God's.

"As my Father sends me, so I am sending you." To do what? To preach the Good News. The Good News is the incarnation, life, crucifixion, resurrection of Jesus Christ, and the affirmation of the new covenant: Love your God with your whole heart, your whole mind, your whole soul;

and love your neighbour as yourself. He said, "By this you shall be known as my disciples: that you love one another as I have loved you". So: "As my Father sent me, so I am sending you. Show them that you are my disciples. Love one another as I have loved you".

The Holy Spirit comes as Fire and Wind to cleanse the heart so there is no impediment for God to pass through.

Whether we are rich or poor, learned or unlearned—there are so many services to be done. Even those who are sick or incapacitated in some way show the features of Christ; there is a "usefulness of uselessness". After all, the most useful hours that Christ spent on this earth were on the cross, though they seem utterly useless from our pragmatic point of view.

These are the verities that the Holy Spirit will bring to us. Let us open ourselves not only to the Wind that blows away all leaves and all trash, but also to the Fire that burns and cleanses at the same time. We can have the Fire and the Wind touch us, because that is what the Holy Spirit came for.

All Made New

The Holy Spirit "makes all things new". We co-operate by opening ourselves, each one of us individually, to this fire of his that will make us "new."

What does it mean to open oneself to the Spirit? It means to allow ourselves to fall completely and utterly into the hands of God. It is said, "It is a terrible thing to fall into the hands of the living God!" So it is, if we read

113

the Scriptures attentively with an open heart and an open mind, and ponder over the love of those who opened themselves totally to God. Like the prophets of old. Like John the Baptist. Like the apostles after the first Pentecost. Like Our Lady with her *Fiat* (Let it be done to me as you will)—her tremendous, constantly renewed *Fiat*. Like the martyrs of the early Church. Like the saints of all ages. To open oneself to God means to open oneself to love, to allow the Spirit to impenetrate us totally and completely.

The Holy Spirit is the fiery furnace into which I must step in order to burn with love. The Father loved me so much that he sent Christ, my brother. But it is the Holy Spirit who makes clear to me what Christ said, "You will not understand until the Advocate, whom my Father will send, comes." Any time we have a problem, we go to the Holy Spirit, because one of his functions is to clarify.

In baptism, my ear has been opened to receive the word of God. I receive it into my head, and I use my intellect to apprehend and comprehend this word given to me by Christ. But after having thought it over with God's gift of intellect, I must lay that word into my heart. I wrap it in a linen cloth of deeper faith and I let it lay there until the tip of the Holy Spirit's "wings" touch it. Then I shall receive a light from above, for the Lord told us that the Advocate will come and enlighten us.

The Holy Spirit, the Advocate, the Clarifier, will show me the depth of this word as it applies to me, or to whatever the situation is. I must be silent, because the Spirit comes to a silent heart; he comes in silence until he reaches his point of contact. It is symbolic: the tip of his wing touches my heart. He is God, he is the Third Person. His job in that love affair between God and us is to clarify love, clarify the Father, clarify Christ to me.

There must be an active part to my reception of the word; that is, my brain acts. And then there must be a passive part.

So, I have laid that word in my heart and soul, and I take it out again after I have waited passively for God the Holy Spirit to come and clarify. How does he clarify? Factually, it is difficult to express because every person has a different reaction.

For myself, I suddenly have a thought about this word that I laid there. It is a new thought that I never had before, or that is an enlargement of what I thought before. Now I am attentive, and I listen with my heart and my soul. Then I take that additional clarification out and I think about it with my brain, plus illumination from faith. And I have new light. And then I lay it back again, because a word is a long time with God: it is a long time growing, a long time lying in the passive, dark depths of my soul before it finally comes to new growth.

The Holy Spirit fills my heart with faith.

Pentecost is the season of hope; it is all about hope. But if I do not believe, then I do not hope. This is the season of hope because the Holy Spirit reveals to us things that we barely dare to believe. One of the risks that a Christian must take is hope. Today we have people who are creating chaos all around the world; it is in bad shape all over the place. But that is where the resurgence of hope comes.

Today my heart is filled with hope because, in the mercy of God, all things are possible.

What is hope? It is faith in things unseen, And how do you get this faith? The only way you get it is from a Flame and a Fire! It is kindled in you by knowing Christ and his Father and the Holy Spirit.

In John's Gospel quoted above, the resurrected Jesus "breathed" on his apostles. What does one do with the breath of God? For it is ours, too; he breathed on his apostles, but all of us are breathed upon in the sacrament of Confirmation. So what does one do with the breath of God?

If God has us "breathe" him in, then we have to breathe him out, because nothing that God gives us is only for me myself alone, but is for everybody. If this is the hour of hope, then nothing matters really, except loving one another. Let us risk everything, even our lives, so that we might love one another, so that we might be compassionate to one another. We just cannot sit back, we to whom the grace of God is given, and leave anyone that we come across lonely or sad. We just cannot. And let us forgive one another, which is part of loving.

Let us love one another, for God is Love. Even when all appears hopeless, nothing is hopeless to us Christians.

Pain and Unity

Few have written on the pain of the first Pentecost, nor of its fears. It must have been a tremendous, fearsome, awesome, painful experience—painful for the human, emotional, intellectual entities that were the apostles, like you and I—to hear this Wind. To see and feel these miraculous tongues of fire fall through a roof that must have been solid and well-timbered. What was their state when those tongues of fire touched their heads? No one knows, but one can surmise, meditate on and contemplate that first Pentecost.

How afraid the apostles must have been when Jesus ascended. Oh yes, he promised not to leave them orphans, but they did not understand. Many times they did not understand, nor do we. So many times he speaks in our hearts and we discard his soft voice, we either miss it or discard it.

Who was this Advocate, this promised Holy Spirit? Who was this strange person who would not leave them orphans after he who was their whole life had left? They could not understand. So for 10 days they cringed at the feet of Our Lady in the upper room. "Cringed" is the word. They were afraid of the Sanhedrin; they were afraid of the Pharisees and the Sadducees, of the Romans—everybody in authority. They were afraid of their own people. So they cringed. But there was one good thing about that cringing: they prayed with Our Lady. Then one day—the day we call Pentecost, the day of the Spirit—they heard the roaring of a great wind.

Did it ever occur to you that God has often come in the wind? He talked to Adam and Eve in the soft breeze of evening. He also came to Elijah (who had expected him to come roaring like thunder) in a gentle wind. And if you listen well he will come to you, usually in a gentle wind.

But at Pentecost the wind was roaring indeed—it shook the place. Their fears grew. Then out of the wind came fire! Yes, tongues of fire, and they rested upon the heads of the apostles and Our Lady. The Promised One had arrived, the Third Person of the Most Holy Trinity, he whom Jesus called the Advocate, the Consoler.

So you have a Father; you have a Brother; you have a Consoler. Moreover, you have a Mother—Our Lady of the Most Holy Trinity. I think of Our Lady as being in the midst of the Trinity. I see the Trinity as movement, fire, and peace. And she who is the spouse of the Holy Spirit, the mother of Jesus Christ, and the daughter of the Father, it seems obvious to me, must be in their midst.

What is "in their midst", when the Most Holy Trinity embraces not only our poor little planet but all the spheres and galaxies and constellations? The dark void is no void to the Trinity; all is light, because all is embraced by them.

When I say "in the midst," I see all of us who are baptized in the resurrected Christ. I see others there too, because Jesus died for all people, of all faiths or none. If we could see with the eyes of God we would see them wending their way down the road of history. Whether they know it or not, all are moving into the resurrected Christ. All are being greeted by the Lord of history whose arms are outstretched to receive them, even as the father did in the case of the Prodigal Son.

The Father, Son, and Holy Spirit are united by the bond of a love beyond our understanding. They are so united that they are One in Three, and Three in One. Here we see the soil from which unity springs, with roots buried deeply in the soil of the Most Holy Trinity.

And we must be united to them. Our brother Jesus Christ, with his incarnation, death, and resurrection, made it possible for us to be one in the Father and with one another, made it possible to transplant some of the roots growing in the bosom of the Trinity into our hearts. The Holy Spirit "waters", as a garden, that unity with the Trinity and with all people, forever watching that all is watered.

We have free will to let the plant of unity die, but what a tragedy! We see the Consoler who holds the water that will revive the plant, and we can ask for this sign of his consolation. Or we can say we do not need it, that we can make it alone. If we do so, Our Lady's tears wash the plant, but she cannot restore unity among us unless we want it restored, because we are created free. We can reject the Trinity: we can reject God the Father; we can reject our Brother; we can reject the Consoler; we can gather the tears of Our Lady and throw them away. Such is our power, we who are created in the image and likeness of God.

But those of us who believe in him, who follow him, who are baptized, we can reflect the face of the Father as we walk the path of the Lord Jesus Christ. And we can rest in the "arms" of the Holy Spirit, for we will need consolation. We will need to hold the hands of Our Lady to keep this unity.

Pentecost, in a manner of speaking, has never stopped since that first Pentecost. The tongues of fire have been falling on Christians ever since—not only on the day of our Confirmation but always, constantly, through the gifts of the Holy Spirit and the graces sent by God. The fact that today the fire is invisible is neither here nor there. The tragedy is that our hearts have grown cold and our faith cold with them. And so the eyes of our souls are sealed, as are its ears, and few hear the immense Wind that constantly blows across humanity. Few of us "see" the Fire that descends in tongues, without ceasing, upon the peoples of God.

Unless I open my heart, my soul and my mind to the searing, burning, miraculous, wondrous fire of the Holy Spirit, I shall not produce the fruits that God so passionately wants me to produce.

Book 5

Madonna House Customs and Traditions

The Season of Lent

Before Lent begins, we take time to get into the spirit of what it is about, to talk about it before it happens.

A week or so before Ash Wednesday, we collect our blessed palm or cedar branches which we had used in the previous year's Palm Sunday procession. (These blessed branches are considered sacramentals, traditionally kept in homes during the year.) These branches are burned, and the resulting ashes will be used in the ceremony of the blessing of our foreheads on Ash Wednesday.

Mardi Gras, literally "Fat Tuesday", the day before Ash Wednesday, is a kind of "farewell" before embarking on the rigors of Lenten practices. The original purpose of Mardi Gras was to use up any rich food in the house before the beginning of the fast, so as not to have tempting left-overs about. Catherine remembered that in Russia meat, dairy products, and all animal fat were given up for Lent. Thus a traditional meal for "Fat Tuesday" was a pancake supper, incorporating some of these foods. We continue this tradition in Madonna House with pancakes and all the trimmings on this day.

This Tuesday is also known as "Shrove Tuesday". The word "shrove" originally referred to the Sacrament of Confession, which was known as shriving a person of their sins. Since repentance is a focal point of Lent, on Shrove Tuesday we encourage everyone to prepare by availing themselves of the Sacrament of Reconciliation. We try to keep Shrove Tuesday evening a quiet one, to interiorly prepare with soul, mind, and body for entering the holy season on the morrow.

At Madonna House in Combermere, even as our minds and hearts are gradually getting molded into an anticipation of the penance of the season, we prepare our neo-Christian version of a Mardi Gras celebration. This involves a party atmosphere, a last fling as it were, before settling into the serious work of Lent. We have traditionally put on a talent show, sometimes called the "Pre–Lent Event", or the "Ash Bash". It involves music, humor, drama, any talent, and everyone here at the time is welcome to participate. This is usually the weekend before Ash Wednesday, so as to enjoy the merriment and still have time to get recollected and ready to begin Lent in earnest on Ash Wednesday morning.

Catherine remembered, "Lent in Russia was really something deep and profound, and people cherished it as a simple and direct way to God. Lent had a very special place in the life of Russians. They made sure that they participated in it and took it upon themselves. In the Eastern rites, catechism is taught through the liturgy. Liturgy is like a mystery play: through the prayers, through whatever is happening, you sense the mystery and the symbolism of things. It is touchable; you can feel it; you respond to it—and not just emotionally. The Russian feels that monotony in the Lenten liturgy creates a climate. Monotony is not good for all year long, but it is good for a little while because it brings an awareness into the heart.

"For many years I lived my Eastern spirituality, and spoke and wrote about it in a childlike way from what I had learned from my parents, my society and culture. But

I did not know the exact background of it all. Then I discovered Fr. Alexander Schmemann's book, *Great Lent*[1], and I realized where this spirituality came from. Fr. Schmemann articulates what I lived."

Catherine often used this book for our Lenten spiritual reading in Combermere, and throughout the Apostolate we continue to utilize it for our Lenten journeys. It opened doors for her and for us to continue to plumb the Eastern heritage of her life that she has passed on to us as an essential part of our Madonna House life. We drink in the Russian "attitudes" of Lent, and incorporate much of the spirit into our apostolic lives

Two examples may demonstrate this.

Each day at the end of Morning Prayer, we pray the following "Prayer of St. Ephrem the Syrian":

Kneel
O Lord, Master of my life, grant that I may not be infected with the spirit of slothfulness and faint-heartedness, with the spirit of ambition and vain talking. *Prostration*
Grant instead to me your servant the spirit of purity and humility, the spirit of patience and love. *Prostration*
O Lord and King, bestow upon me the grace of being aware of my sins and of not judging my brother, for you are blessed forever. Amen. *Stand*
O God, purify me a sinner and have mercy on me. *Repeat 3 times with a metania.*[2] *Then kneel.*

---

1   New York: St. Vladimir's Seminary Press, revised 1974
2   *Metania* or *metany* comes from the Greek word *metanoia*. This gesture involves a bow at the waist, touching the floor before or after—according to various traditions—signing yourself with the cross.

Yes, O Lord and King, bestow upon me the grace of being aware of my sins and of not judging my .brother. *Prostration*

Catherine again, "After each petition we prostrate our bodies, touching our heads to the floor according to the Eastern tradition. Why do Eastern people prostrate themselves? Because we have such a sense of who we are, and who God is. A Russian prostrates to acknowledge that he is a creature and God is God; and a creature's proper position is prone. All idea of my importance, my greatness, my intellectual or spiritual capacity vanish when I am prostrate, or so we Easterners think. (What also happens is that you get a great suppleness of body that is retained into old age!)"

The second example is the hymn with which we begin our Morning Prayer, "Open to Me the Doors of Repentance":

Open to me the doors of repentance O Lifegiver
For my spirit rises early to pray towards thy holy temple
Bearing the temple of my body all defiled
But in thy compassion purify me by the loving kindness
of thy mercy.

Lead me on the paths of salvation O Mother of God
For I have profaned my soul with shameful sins,
and have wasted my life in laziness.
But by your intercessions deliver me from all impurity.

Have mercy on me O God, according to thy great mercy
And according to the multitude of thy compassions,
blot out my transgressions.

When I think of the many evil things I have done,
wretch that I am,
I tremble at the fearful day of judgment.

But trusting in thy loving kindness,
like David I cry to thee:
Have mercy on me O God, have mercy on me O God,
Have mercy on me O God, according to thy great mercy.

The hymns and prayers of Lent, from both East and West, feed our spirits in a profound way as we pray Mass and the Office.

There are other Lenten customs we practice which any one can adapt to their lives.

We read aloud together the readings of the Sunday liturgy, to discuss and pray with; we invite friends to share in this. We look for spiritual books appropriate to the season for personal and communal reading. The book Catherine mentions above, *Great Lent*, is a favorite choice.

We eat more simply, cutting back on extras. Besides fasting from food, we can "fast" from light reading, television and radio, and in this day and age, our use of the computer. There are endless ways to fast! And there is almsgiving, along with prayer and fasting, one of *the* traditional activities of Lent. With our promise of poverty in Madonna House, "alms of the heart" are more common than the alms of money: tenderness with one another, forgiveness, a kind word. There are also the "alms of service" to others, especially hidden services. Such "alms" are an essential aspect of anyone's Lent.

Displays or decorations focus on Lenten themes, especially utilizing Scripture. For example, we would letter a poster or scroll with quotes such as the following: "Repent and believe the good news.", "Rend your hearts and not your garments." Or later in Lent, "By his wounds we are healed."

Another custom Catherine encouraged was making or "writing" the Easter eggs known as *pysanky*. We start making these as soon as Lent begins. We blow out the insides of raw eggs (with the contents going to our meals). Designs are "written" onto the eggs with an instrument called a *kistka*, described as a "pen which writes with melted wax"[3]. The eggs are dipped sequentially in various colors of dye, from lightest to darkest, with the waxed areas "resisting" the new colors. At the end of the dyeing process, all the wax is melted off, and the beautiful multi-colored egg is revealed. We sometimes describe this process as one of moving from light to darkness, and then darkness to light, and thus truly symbolizing this season of Lent and Resurrection. There are a number of books easily available which demonstrate the process and show the traditional designs of pysanky.

We have carried this tradition to our field houses all over the world, teaching people from Arizona to Quebec, to Belgium and Russia, even in Africa, how to make pysanky. People are very moved by the symbolism of these eggs, as well as the many designs with their Christian meanings. It is very important to make pysanky as a Christian project; we consider it a "graced" activity of the season in its own way. The finished eggs are fragile, but they can be saved from year to year.

There is a wonderful tradition behind pysanky making which we have made our own: Should the custom cease, evil will encompass and destroy the world, because evil is seen as heavily chained, and the fewer decorated eggs, the looser become the chains, and evil begins to flow through the world. But the more eggs decorated, the tighter the

---

3   *Eggs Beautiful: How to Make Ukrainian Easter Eggs* by Johanna Luciow, Ann Kmit, Loretta Luciow. Minneapolis, MN: Ukrainian Gift Shop

chains become, and evil is again pushed back.[4] Each year we do our part to keep evil from triumphing!

In many places we also craft our own Paschal candle. We melt stubs of beeswax candles, and pour the wax into a cylindrical mould. The carving into the candle of the liturgical symbols makes a wonderful contemplative Lenten activity.

Holy Week Customs

Holy Week in Russia

Catherine writes about Holy Week in the Russia of her youth, "As Holy Week drew near, the atmosphere throughout Russia became more intense. All thoughts were with the Lord in his passion and crucifixion. Lent had been a preparation for Easter—Life had slowed down, become subdued.

"Yet every free minute had been used for preparing physically for the great day of the Resurrection. In our mentality, two things went with spiritual festivals of this type. First, an immaculate house: a person might have been as poor as a church mouse, but she would not eat, so as to buy soap to clean the house. God comes on Resurrection day in a very special way to each house, through family and guests. Thus everything had to be spotless.

"Second, no matter how poor anyone was, they would also save up in order to have some goodies or sweet foods,

---

4   Ibid.

because Christ is sweet, 'sweeter than honey in the honeycomb'.

"We tasted the sweetness of God by eating the traditional Easter foods, paska and koolitch.

"The koolitch, an especially rich bread, required a lot of kneading. Each family member took a hand; the children shelled the almonds and cleaned the raisins.

"Paska is a white dessert symbolizing Christ. Mainly of cottage cheese, mixed with honey, butter, and raisins, it was drained and put into a mold with a cross clearly etched on each of its four sides and the initials of Jesus Christ carved into it. The cook put quite a bit of honey or sugar into that paska, so that those who had fasted for forty days could re–taste, after the supper of the Lord, how sweet he is!

"Finally, the Easter eggs to be eaten were dyed and decorated. All Easter foods had symbolic significance to the people of my country. But Easter eggs formed the core, the heart, of the breaking of the Lenten fast following the Easter liturgy in Russia. For eggs were the symbol of eternal life, of the new life lived in Christ. The egg, being the embodiment of the life principle, is a symbol of our rebirth in Christ through baptism. It was also likened to the tomb from which Christ arose.

"The egg was the first of the Easter foods to be blessed by the priest; even the poorest of the poor, who perhaps could not afford any other Easter foods, would have decorated and dyed eggs to bring to the Church for blessing. It was with these that the long fast of the Easter Vigil, and of Lent, was broken.

"Easter eggs were given as Easter gifts. They spoke to us of the Parousia, Christ's second coming, and of our final resurrection into a life of love and joy and eternal union with him. Easter eggs are an extension of the liturgy, understood, participated in, and lived. They are part of the tremendous love story between God and man."

Holy Week and the Triduum

On one of the evenings of Holy Week, we dye the hard boiled eggs which we will use to break the fast after the Easter Vigil liturgy. As Catherine reminds us above, eggs symbolize new life, eternal life, and are a special Easter food. Catherine encouraged us to "let the dyeing of eggs be a little party." So in Madonna House, in the midst of the liturgical solemnity of Holy Week, this evening of egg dyeing is a light family time, giving a little glimpse of the joy and light to come.

Holy Week is also a good time to confess one's sins before the great feast. In Combermere, we have a communal penance service on one of the nights before the Triduum.

Holy Thursday begins the *Triduum*—the three holiest days of the liturgical year. The evening meal, prior to the Evening Mass of the Lord's Supper, is a solemn one with white tablecloths and candles. In Madonna House we call this meal the "Supper of the Lamb" We traditionally serve foods symbolic of the feast, rooted in the Passover supper of our Jewish ancestors in the faith: lamb, bread, wine. In Combermere our farm has raised and saved an unblemished male yearling sheep. It is roasted, and carried whole by men staff around the main dining room before it is served. This ceremony symbolizes Christ, the Lamb who was slain for our sake.

Before the meal begins, the history and meaning of the events we are celebrating are explained. We read about the Hebrew Passover from the book of Exodus (12:1–14). At the end of the meal, we read from St. John's Gospel, "The Priestly Prayer of Jesus". These are Jesus's intimate words to his Father on our behalf. The very formality of the meal sets this day apart from all other days.[5]

Good Friday is, of course, a day of silence, recollection, prayer and com-passion with the Lord. At the same time, it holds within itself the joy of Easter, for on the spiritual horizon, the Son of Easter is rising. In Madonna House, as in the universal Church, it is a day of fast and abstinence and of mortification—personal and collective.

Only hot cross buns are served at breakfast, with tea and coffee, and sometimes honey. We have a simple midday meal, and for supper we serve only boiled potatoes.

The hot cross buns should be fairly highly spiced with cinnamon, nutmeg, etc. These spices symbolize the myrrh and other aromatics that were used in the burial of Christ. A cross is made on the top of the buns, either in the dough or with icing. This reminds us of both the cross and the tomb. (Incidentally, hot cross buns also could be made every Friday throughout Lent because of this symbolism.)

In contrast to the festive table of Holy Thursday, on Good Friday our tables are left bare, with only a plain

---

5   For a text of Madonna House's "Supper of the Lamb", see Appendix

wooden cross in the center of each. Other decorations reflecting Good Friday can be placed around the house.

In Combermere, on the evening of Good Friday we are privileged to participate in the Byzantine liturgical celebration of the "Office of the Burial of Christ". This is "a meditation on the Savior's entombment and on his descent into Hades to save the souls of the just and open for them the gates of heaven....The time Christ remained in the tomb is seen as a period of refreshing sleep after the sufferings of the Passion, and as a prelude to the victory of the Resurrection."[6]

This is a beautiful service of songs and prayers and symbols, not only of the suffering of our Savior, but also the light of the resurrection beginning to shine from the tomb. Archbishop Joseph Raya introduced Madonna House to this celebration, and we have come to love it very much. In our field houses, we also assist at this service if there is a Byzantine church in our area.

On **Holy Saturday** a large, bare, rough wooden cross, draped with a purple or white cloth is the focal display in the Combermere dining room. Three nails are placed at the foot of it, and a crown of thorns at the crossbar. This is our only decor; we do not use scrolls with wording, in order to echo the silence of the tomb. Throughout the day we preserve an atmosphere of respectful and expectant silence.

---

6   *Byzantine Daily Worship*, Archbishop Joseph Raya and Baron Jose de Vinck, Alleluia Press, 1969

We Celebrate Easter!

We break our Lenten fast with the traditional Easter foods of eggs, paska and koolitch. Of course we share these foods with guests and visitors. They demonstrate in a physical way the symbolism of this greatest feast and truth of our faith.

Koolitch is a sweet yeast bread, baked in high round loaves (coffee cans make good molds). For the simplest celebration, one loaf is baked high, representing Christ; one is baked a little lower, representing his bride the Church. To complete the koolitch baking, we form the letters *P A X*, "peace", out of dough. This was the greeting of Christ to those he encountered after his resurrection. In our Combermere training center, we also bake one loaf representing Our Lady, and 12 loaves representing the apostles.

Paska takes its name from the word *Pasch*, from the Hebrew for Passover. It is primarily made from cottage cheese, mixed with the special ingredients Catherine describes above, foods from which we have fasted during Lent. The paska symbolizes Christ as the pure and innocent Lamb of God, the Lamb who was slain for the salvation of the world. The paska reminds us of the richness and sweetness of our redemption. We share this special food throughout the apostolate as part of the festive board of Easter.

In Madonna House we have our festive collation, or meal, right after the Easter Vigil liturgy. The koolitch, paska, and eggs dyed earlier in the week are blessed by the priest, according to the Roman Ritual's "Blessings of Food at Easter".

When everyone is gathered around the table, each takes first a colored egg. Turning to his neighbor at the table, he hits the neighbor's egg with his egg (a manner of toasting) saying: "Christ is Risen!" The other person replies: "Verily (or truly) he is Risen!" They then embrace each other three times, kissing each other's cheek, or laying one cheek against another. The ceremony is repeated from one to another. This is the Christian "Kiss of Peace" of the old days of the a*gape*.

Then the tall koolitch is cut—the one that symbolizes Christ—and the first "breaking of the fast" is done by eating a piece of the egg and the koolitch, with a little bit of the paska which has also been dished out. (The paska should be barely tasted, as it is supposed to be a dessert to finish up the meal. It is used at the beginning of the meal only symbolically.)

The rest of the foods such as ham, or other kinds of meat and fowl, salads, etc., are just a pleasant addition and have no symbolic significance.

Some may wonder why we have our special foods. It seems we are losing the connection between a great event like Easter, Christmas, and other holy days, and the celebrations that accompany them. We are losing the connection between the holy mystery of the liturgy and another mystery called *agape*—the breaking of bread in mutual love and celebration. We should have special foods, as well as flowers or other special decorations, to show that this is a big event.

Madonna House has accumulated some joyous, beautiful, heart–lifting traditions and customs which bring forth the spirit of the feast.

At any moment during the meal (or any meal during Easter week) we may break out into song as someone feels moved to lead us in singing the triumphant Byzantine Easter hymn: "Christ is risen from the dead, trampling down death by his death; and upon those in the tombs, lavishing life!" We accompany this by clinking of glasses and ringing of as many little hand bells as we can locate! It is a time of new life.

At supper on Easter Sunday, or at another supper in Easter week, we read aloud the wonderful "Resurrection Homily of St. John Chrysostom".

Let all pious men and all lovers of God rejoice in the splendor of this feast; let the wise servants blissfully enter into the joy of their Lord; let those who have borne the burden of Lent now receive their pay, and those who have toiled since the first hour, let them now receive their due reward; let any who came after the third hour be grateful to join in the feast, and those who may have come after the sixth, let them not be afraid of being too late, for the Lord is gracious and He receives the last even as he first. He gives rest to him who comes on the eleventh hour as well as to him who has toiled since the first: yes, He has pity on the last and He serves the first; He rewards the one and is generous to the other; he repays the deed and praises the effort.

Come you all: enter into the joy of your Lord. You the first and you the last, receive alike your reward; you rich and you poor, dance together; you sober and you weaklings, celebrate the day; you who have kept the fast and you who have not, rejoice today. The table is richly loaded: enjoy its royal banquet. The calf is a fatted one: let no one go away hungry.

All of you enjoy the banquet of faith; all of you receive the riches of his goodness. Let no one grieve over his poverty, for the universal kingdom has been revealed; let no one weep over his sins, for pardon has shone from the grave; let no one fear death, for the death of our Saviour has set us free: He has destroyed it by enduring it, He has despoiled Hades by going down into its kingdom, He has angered it by allowing it to taste of his flesh...

Hades is angered because frustrated, it is angered because it has been mocked, it is angered because it has been destroyed, it is angered because it has been reduced to naught, it is angered because it is now captive. It seized a body, and, lo! It discovered God; it seized death, and, behold! It encountered heaven; it seized the visible, and was overcome by the invisible.

O death, where is your sting? O Hades, where is your victory? Christ is risen and you are abolished, Christ is risen and the demons are cast down, Christ is risen and the angels rejoice, Christ is risen and life is freed, Christ is risen and the tomb is emptied of the dead: for Christ, being risen from the dead, has become the Leader and Reviver of those who had fallen asleep. To Him be glory and power for ever and ever. Amen.[7]

The whole eight days or octave, beginning on Easter Sunday, are traditionally considered to be *one single day*— Resurrection Day—so great is this feast. Special foods are served all week during this day of days. In fact, all during the seven weeks of the Easter season extra treat foods are

7   *Byzantine Daily Worship*, Archbishop Joseph Raya and Baron Jose de Vinck, Alleluia Press, 1969, pp 859-60.

served impromptu, as part of celebrating Christ's resurrection, and the promise of our own. And of course we
continue singing the exuberant Easter hymns.

Not least in the way of Madonna House family customs at Easter, is time off from work. For three days no
one does any work other than the essential tasks, such as
cooking, care of the sick, liturgical preparations, and for
our farmers, animal care. We can be with each other,
almost oblivious to time, living already, in a sense, in a bit
of the heaven Christ has re–opened to us. This is one more
practice which helps us to really feel and enter into the
significance of the feast.

Pentecost Customs

The feast of Pentecost is the final day of the Easter season. Each day of the week preceding we prepare for it as
a community at Morning Prayer (Lauds): the person leading prayers includes an explanation of one of the seven
gifts of the Holy Spirit: fear of the Lord, piety, fortitude,
counsel, knowledge, understanding, and wisdom. (See
Isaiah 11:2.)

We also reflect on the twelve fruits of the Holy Spirit:
love, joy, peace, patience, kindness, goodness, generosity,
gentleness, faithfulness, modesty, chastity, and self-con-
trol. (See Galatians 5:22.)

For those who will be present at supper on Pentecost,
we prepare "gifts", cutting paper into a shape symbolic of
the feast, such as tongues of fire or doves, one for each
person. On the front of each is written one of the seven
gifts of the Holy Spirit; and on the reverse, one of the
fruits of the Spirit, in random combinations. The papers

are placed in a basket and well mixed. During supper we sing a hymn to the Holy Spirit as each person draws a gift. Each then shares with all what gift or fruit they have received.

Catherine taught us, "this custom is very important. I would like to impress on the members of the Apostolate that they have to take the gift and fruit they receive as coming from God. They must bestir themselves to practice them most diligently; they should also do some private reading and research into the depths of a given gift or fruit. It would not hurt members to have sort of a double joy in having to meditate on and practice, implement into their lives, a gift of the Holy Spirit and a fruit stemming from it." This custom helps us to appreciate the gifts and fruits and foster their growth in us.

For Pentecost we make other preparations as usual for feast days: we cook festive foods; decorate the tables and the house with symbolic creations, such as a hanging mobile of paper "tongues of fire", posters, or red candles; we select and practice hymns that beautifully express the meaning of the feast; and choose spiritual readings that relate the feast to our daily life.

The day after Pentecost, we return to Ordinary Time in the Liturgical Year. As we live the whole liturgical year as a family, we realize that in order to celebrate feast days well, we must live in marked simplicity and plainness during Ordinary Time; then the feast days will stand out in contrast. In other words, the plainness of Ordinary Time helps us to relish the exuberance of feast days.

The rhythm of alternating periods of ordinariness and celebration is constantly in play in many aspects of our life: food; liturgy and liturgical music; home decorations; the way we dress—dressing up for Sundays and feasts—and free time. During Lent we emphasize the plainness and monotony even more than in Ordinary Time, and strain toward the ecstatic joy of celebrating Christ's resurrection, which heralds our own.

Appendix

The Supper of the Lamb

1. *Introduction*: We call this meal the "Supper of the Lamb". Christ, the Lamb of God, is slain for us. Joyfully, in love, He gives his very life—His blood—for the salvation of the world. He allows Himself to be the victim in our place, obedient to His Father "even unto death."

It is the custom in the Jewish household for the mother of the home to inaugurate Sabbath festivities by the lighting of the Sabbath candles. The observance of this precept was said to ensure domestic peace and to bring the light of sanctity to the home. In our supper we are gathered together by the One who is Light of the Father's Light—Jesus Christ, forever the light of the world.

2. Before *lighting the candelabrum*, the mother of the house prays: "Blessed are you, O Lord our God, King of the Universe. You make us holy by the light of your Son, Jesus Christ."

3. *Continue with explanation* and blessing:

The Gospel of St. Mark says: "On the first day of Unleavened Bread, when the Passover Lamb was sacrificed, His disciples said to Jesus, 'Where do you want us to go to make preparations for you to eat the Passover?'"

We gather tonight to prepare for the Eucharistic celebration of this Last Supper, which the Lord celebrated with His disciples. On that night, in a Jewish Passover meal, he broke bread and gave it to them saying, "This is my Body." He took wine, blessed it and gave it to them saying, "This is my Blood."

We gather with Jesus and all His disciples on this night in which He begins His passion. By so doing, we are drawn into the Mystery of mysteries: The Lord Jesus's passing over to his Father, the pouring out of His own life-blood for us.

First in this symbolic meal and later in the sacred reality of the liturgy, we celebrate this sacrificial moment in the life of the Lord Jesus. Through the gift of the Eucharist it becomes our moment, and it transforms us. We enter into Christ's death so as to pass with Him into life eternal in the Father and the Holy Spirit.

Blessing:

Blessed are you, God of all creation. You have given us the earth, and food to eat and wine to drink. Bless these gifts with the power of your Spirit that they may sustain us in our journey.

Blessed are you, God and Father of our Lord Jesus Christ, You have given us your only Son, Jesus. He has given us his own body and blood as our food and drink.

Bless us with your Spirit that this meal we now share may remind us of the love that has saved us and made us one. We ask you this through the same Christ, Our Lord.

4. *Lamb is brought in* as opening verses of Psalm 135/136 are sung or said. "Oh give thanks to the Lord for he is good..."

5. *Reading* of the paschal homily by St. Melito of Sardis:[1]

---

1   Office of Readings for Holy Thursday, *The Liturgy of the Hours, Vol. II, Lenten Season, Easter Season.* New York: Catholic Book Publishing Co., 1976

"The Lamb that was slain has delivered us from death and given us life.

"There was much proclaimed by the prophets about the mystery of the Passover: that mystery is Christ, and to him be glory for ever and ever. Amen.

"For the sake of suffering humanity he came down from heaven to earth, clothed himself in that humanity in the Virgin's womb, and was born a man. Having then a body capable of suffering, he took the pain of fallen man upon himself; he triumphed over the diseases of soul and body that were its cause, and by his Spirit, which was incapable of dying, he dealt man's destroyer, death, a fatal blow.

"He was led forth like a lamb; he was slaughtered like a sheep. He ransomed us from our servitude to the world, as he had ransomed Israel from the hand of Egypt; he freed us from our slavery to the devil, as he had freed Israel from the hand of Pharaoh. He sealed our souls with his own Spirit and the members of our body with his own blood.

"He is the One who covered death with shame and cast the devil into mourning, as Moses cast Pharaoh into mourning. He is the One who smote sin and robbed iniquity of offspring, as Moses robbed the Egyptians of their offspring. He is the One who brought us out of slavery into freedom, out of darkness into light, out of death into life, out of tyranny into an eternal kingdom; who made us a new priesthood, a people chosen to be his own for ever. He is the Passover that is our salvation.

"It is he who endured every kind of suffering in all those who foreshadowed him. In Abel he was slain, in

Isaac bound, in Jacob exiled, in Joseph sold, in Moses exposed to die. He was sacrificed in the Passover lamb, persecuted in David, dishonored in the prophets.

"It is he who was made man of the Virgin, he who was hung on the tree; it is he who was buried in the earth, raised from the dead, and taken up to the heights of heaven. He is the mute lamb, the slain lamb, the lamb born of Mary the fair ewe. He was seized from the flock, dragged off to be slaughtered, sacrificed in the evening, buried at night. On the tree no bone of his was broken; in the earth his body knew no decay. He is the One who rose from the dead, and who raised man from the depths of the tomb."

6. Further verses of Psalm 135/136 are said or sung as lamb is carried back out to the kitchen.

7. *Blessing before beginning to eat*: Now let us celebrate with the Lord Jesus and His disciples. Let us enter into fellowship with Him, who held nothing of Himself from us.

8. At the end of the meal we read from the Lord's last discourse to His disciples. These are the verses from the Gospel of St. John we use at Madonna House:

John 13: 31,33-35; 14:1-3, 6-7, 23, 27; 15:9-17; 16:12-15a, 20-24, 33; 17:1-3, 6-7, 17-26

9. *Dismissal:* after a moment of silence, a leader prays: "Let us go forth to enter into the Lord's Passover in peace and joy."

About the Author

Catherine de Hueck Doherty was born in Russia on August 15, 1896, and baptized in the Russian Orthodox Church. Because of her father's work, she grew up in Ukraine, Egypt, and Paris as well as Russia. Many different strands of Christianity were woven into the spiritual fabric of her family background, but it was from the liturgy of the Orthodox Church, the living faith of her father and mother, and the earthy piety of the Russian people themselves that Catherine received the powerful spiritual traditions and symbols of the Christian East.

At fifteen Catherine was married to Boris de Hueck. Soon they were swept into World War I, where she served as a nurse at the front. On their return to St. Petersburg, she and Boris barely escaped the turmoil of the Russian Revolution, nearly starving to death as refugees in Finland. Eventually they made their way to England, where Catherine was received into the Catholic Church.

Emigrating to Canada with Boris, Catherine gave birth to their only child, George, in 1921 in Toronto. As refugees, they experienced dire poverty for a few years. But soon Catherine's intelligence, energy, and gift for public speaking brought her to the attention of a large lecture bureau. Her talks were popular all across Canada and the United States, and within a few years, she became an executive.

In the 1930's, after several years of anguish, Catherine and Boris separated permanently; later the Church annulled their marriage. As devastated as Catherine was, she knew that God wanted something new from her now.

The words of Christ haunted her: "Sell all you possess, and give it to the poor, and come, follow Me." She consulted the archbishop of Toronto about her new vocation, and began her lay apostolate among the poor in Toronto in the early 1930's, calling it Friendship House.

Because her approach was so different from what was being done at the time, she encountered much persecution and resistance, and Friendship House was forced to close in 1936. Later she was given the chance to revive Friendship House among the poor in Harlem in New York City. This work eventually expanded to other cities: Chicago, Washington, D.C., and Portland, Oregon. Friendship House became well known in the American Church.

But many could not grasp the largeness of her vision, especially because her experience of the ways of God were so foreign to them. After a painful difference of opinion over the nature of the Friendship House apostolate, Catherine found herself again pushed into the chartless waters of the Lord.

This time, however, she did not have to start alone. In 1943 she had married Eddie Doherty, one of America's foremost reporters, who had fallen in love with her while writing a story about Friendship House. Catherine and Eddie arrrived in Combermere, Ontario, on May 17, 1947. What seemed like the end of the road turned out to be the most fruitful period of Catherine's life. Catherine had a faith vision for the restoration of the Church and our modern culture, which brought lay men and women as well as priests to Madonna House to live a Gospel life in a family called to love like the Holy Family in Nazareth.

The community of Madonna House has continued to grow from those early years.

Catherine Doherty died on December 14, 1985, after a long illness. Her Apostolate now numbers over 200 members, including more than twenty priests, with foundations around the world. She left to the Church, which she loved passionately, a spiritual heritage that is a beacon for this new century, in her writings, and in the community of Madonna House that she founded.

In 1996 the directors of Madonna House petitioned the Bishop of Pembroke, Ontario, the home diocese of Madonna House, to open her cause for canonization. The process is now underway, and Catherine is called "Servant of God".

Other Books by Catherine Doherty

Available through Madonna House Publications

MADONNA HOUSE PUBLICATIONS
COMBERMERE • ONTARIO • CANADA • K0J 1L0

"Lord, give bread to the hungry, and hunger for you to those who have bread," was a favourite prayer of our foundress, Catherine Doherty. At Madonna House Publications, we strive to satisfy the spiritual hunger for God in our modern world with the timeless words of the Gospel message.

Faithful to the teachings of the Catholic Church and its magisterium, Madonna House Publications is a non-profit apostolate dedicated to publishing high quality and easily accessible books, audiobooks, videos and music. We pray our publications will awaken and deepen in our readers an experience of Jesus' love in the most simple and ordinary facets of everyday life.

Your generosity can help Madonna House Publications provide the poor around the world with editions of important spiritual works containing the enduring wisdom of the Gospel message. If you would like to help, please send your contribution to the address below. We also welcome your questions and comments. May God bless you for your participation in this apostolate.

Madonna House Publications
2888 Dafoe Rd, RR 2
Combermere ON   K0J 1L0
Canada

Internet: www.madonnahouse.org/publications
E-mail: publications@madonnahouse.org
Telephone: (613) 756-3728